The Man Who Made Things Out of Trees

ROBERT PENN

PENGUIN BOOKS

PENGUIN BOOKS

UK | USA | Canada | Ireland | Australia
India | New Zealand | South Africa

Penguin Books is part of the Penguin Random House group of companies
whose addresses can be found at global.penguinrandomhouse.com.

First published by Particular Books 2015
Published in Penguin Books 2016
001

Copyright © Robert Penn, 2015

The moral right of the author has been asserted

Set in 12/15.38 pt Garamond MT Std
Typeset by Jouve (UK), Milton Keynes
Printed in Great Britain by Clays Ltd, St Ives plc

A CIP catalogue record for this book is available from the British Library

ISBN: 978–0–141–97751–5

Contents

Venus of the Woods

'. . . the Ash for nothing ill'
Edmund Spenser,
The Faerie Queene, Book I

I grew up under an ash tree. It stood over the gate that led from my childhood garden to the fields where my brother and I played out our fantasies. To dash past the elegant, slim-hipped, sweeping form of that ash in winter and to flash beneath its airy canopy in summer was to be transformed into a colonel or a king, a knight or a wizard. That ash was, for many years, the gatekeeper to my dreams.

I can't remember as a child ever making the connection between that tree and many of the things I loved. I don't think I even knew that my prized Dunlop tennis racket, my hockey stick, my cricket stumps and bails, the rocking chair in my brother's bedroom and our toboggan were all made out of ash wood. Yet that tree somehow stuck with me. Ever since then, I have instinctively looked for ash trees in the woodlands and fields, and even in the urban landscapes where I have lived. The presence of the tree was somehow braided into the long journeys I have made around the world. It may even be that this tree was a cardinal point, a lodestar that brought me, at the end of my journeying, to live with my family in a house within a small woodland on the edge of the Black Mountains, South Wales – in a landscape similar to that which I knew as a child, a place where ash grows abundantly.

The woodland is on a south-facing slope. Fields and moorland enclose it on two sides. The Arw stream marks the southern boundary. Mixed deciduous trees, including rarely planted species, are arranged haphazardly. Perhaps trees have stood here for a very long time, but it would be wrong to look at this woodland as something eternal and unchangeable. A woodland only represents the natural order of things at a particular moment in time.

When we moved to our house over a decade ago, no one had raised an axe or swung a billhook here since the Second World War, when much of the woodland in the area was felled to provide timber for the war effort. It was a dark, tangled thicket with a canopy of leaves as carefully stitched as a Welsh quilt. The light was thin. The air was restricted. The woodland was somehow lifeless.

I was unsure about what to do with my wood. Then I reread *A Sand County Almanac* by Aldo Leopold, the early American environmentalist. He wrote: 'I have read many definitions of what is a conservationist, and written not a few myself, but I suspect that the best one is written not with a pen but with an axe.' And, tentatively, one winter I started to coppice – the ancient woodland management practice of cutting trees back to ground level to stimulate regrowth. I felled the old, bulging hazel stools along the field boundaries. I thinned out the weakest trees, rendering new vigour to what was left. I created glades. I planted oak trees. I left standing dead timber and rotting wood on the ground. Birds began to nest in the piles of brash. Wildflowers – a few wood anemones, celandines, stitchwort, yellow archangel, lords and ladies, woodland violets, foxgloves and bluebells – sprung to life.

As I cleared the smaller trees or underwood, the taller trees – the single-stemmed, timber trees called 'maidens' – began to emerge. The skeletal character of individual trees was revealed: the muscularity of the oaks; the stanchion-like alders along the stream; the silver birch with their flamboyant mops of claret-coloured twigs. Most conspicuous of all in the dormant wood were the ash trees: cast in tender light and naked of leaf, they were grey-green barked, sparsely branched, tall, slender and austere with twigs that rose and fell and rose again at their tips to end in the distinctive 'witches' claws', which scratched against the pearl-grey sky. Ash wears the winter with a grace that no other tree species can match, hence its nickname – 'Venus of the Woods'.

The ash or genus *Fraxinus*, one of twenty-four genera in the Oleaceae family, includes some forty-three species, according to Dr Gabriel Hemery, author of *The New Sylva*, and they grow within the temperate and subtropical regions of the northern hemisphere. Three species of ash are native to Europe. Of these, European or common ash (*Fraxinus excelsior*) is by far the most widely distributed and important. Common ash grows from the Atlantic coast of Ireland across Europe to the city of Kazan, five hundred miles east of Moscow. The northernmost limit of its distribution is the Trondheim fjord in Norway at 64 °N. The eastern boundary traces the river Volga to Crimea and the Caucasus. The southern edge of common ash's domain starts around 37 °N in Iran and takes a rough line through Dalmatia, Italy and southern France, to the Pyrenees. On the Iberian Peninsula, common ash only grows in the mountains. As a general rule, common ash is a tree of the mountains in southern Europe: further north, it is a tree of the valleys and plains.

In Britain, ash is the third most common broad-leaved tree, after oak and birch. It thrives best on deep, fertile loam over outcrops of carboniferous limestone, ideally on well-drained, northern and eastern slopes where the atmosphere is moist and cool. Ash won't grow on waterlogged sites but it will tolerate a wide range of climatic conditions, provided the soils are suitable. It grows better in mixed woodland than in pure plantations and is frequent in hedgerows. Ash is also tolerant of air pollution, making it a popular tree in urban parks and gardens. Ash can even survive where there is almost no soil: it grows like scrub on bare, limestone rocks in upland parts of Yorkshire and Derbyshire, shooting from chinks in the paving.

Normally vigorous and dense-rooted, ash makes significant demands on easily available nutrients in the soil. While it is exacting in this respect, ash is generous in others. It is aristocratically late to leaf. The feathery canopy of an ash tree in late spring and summer is fragile and airy, casting a gossamer shade, which permits plenty of light on to the woodland floor. This encourages a rich diversity of ground vegetation, commonly including oxlip, wood anemones, meadowsweet, ransoms and the wildflower that grows in sweet-smelling ponds of mauve and has the power of Prozac on the British collective consciousness in spring – bluebells.

Ash trees begin to bear good seed crops at around thirty years old, with maximum seed production at forty to sixty years. The elliptic winged seed vessels known as 'keys' appear in spring and grow over summer. In autumn, they turn brown and hard. Finally, strong winds and occasionally children pluck them from the branches and scatter them considerable distances.

Ash trees produce millions of these seeds, which can result in staggering displays of self-propagation. Ash is the largest single contributor to natural regeneration in British broad-leaved woodlands. Ash is also a 'pioneer' species and quick to invade vacant ground. Ash seedlings are shade-tolerant and can live in a dwarf state for several years, waiting for a gale or the woodman to fell a neighbouring tree and let the light pour in. On the best sites, growth is then rapid. In good conditions, ash is more productive than oak: trunks of 6 metres in length and 40–60 centimetres in diameter at breast height are reached in fifty years. Growth slows after sixty years or so.

The bark of young ash trees is grey-green, smooth and often overlaid with a tapestry of lichen and moss. With age, the bark cracks to form an irregular pattern of fluted ridges and vertical fissures. Ash bark is less susceptible than the bark of other broad-leaf species to stripping by grey squirrels, who cause untold damage to trees in Britain, Ireland and Italy.

The flower-buds – sooty black, ebullient and flattened at the tip – are unlike the buds on any other tree: they appear impatiently on the previous year's shoots in winter, providing a ready means of identifying the species. Short, dense, greenish-white or purple clusters of flowers are produced in April, though not every year. The species has both male and female reproductive organs. Individual trees will display a range of genders over successive years including male, female and hermaphrodite. Why this is so remains a mystery. After a few weeks, the stamen flowers shrivel and fall, leaving the seed chambers.

The compound, pinnate (from the Latin word *pinnatus* meaning 'feathered') leaves comprise pairs of leaflets placed opposite each other on a central stalk, usually with a single leaflet on the end of the stalk. The leaflets are lance-shaped and 2 to 5 inches long with toothed edges. They are dark green and smooth on top, and paler underneath. Occasionally, the single leaflet on the end of the stalk is absent. The relative rarity of this led to the popular belief that an ash leaf with an even number of leaflets brought good luck: in the Middle Ages, young girls in the north of England hoping to meet a husband would traditionally pluck ash leaves with an even number of leaflets, and keep them in their left shoe.

Single-stem ash trees can live for up to 200 years. Coppicing can extend the life of an ash tree up to 400 years or more and there are many examples of wonderfully misshapen, gnarled, ancient ash 'stools' across Europe. In woodland, ash forms a trunk free of side branches to a great height, often with a substantial girth. In favoured sites, trees can grow to a height of 45 metres. Throughout civilization, though, common ash trees have most frequently been felled and used long before they reach this sort of size. In fact, and most significantly, no other widely distributed European broad-leaf tree becomes so useful, so early in its life.

Ash wood is pinkish white and disturbingly like human skin when freshly sawn. It dries into an attractive, pale, creamy-white timber. Though second in value to oak for much of history, ash – of moderate weight, strong, elastic, easily bent and readily worked – has always been more versatile and functional. Human beings have used ash to make ladders, tent pegs, butcher's blocks, boat hooks, beanpoles, looms, bobbins, sieve rims, fishing rods, landing nets, clothes pegs, clothes props, crutches, crates for transporting food, scantlings for stretchers, orthopaedic frames and umbrella handles. During the Middle Ages ash was also used for joists and beams. The best blocks for pulleys and the stays for bells in church towers were made from ash. Ash makes excellent walking sticks and staffs. For much of history, children have known that ash makes first-rate catapults. It makes attractive panelling and flooring, too, and was once a popular choice of timber for pit-props in coal mines.

Ash has been employed to till and cultivate the land for millennia. It has been used to make ploughs, harrows and wheelbarrows. Ash made the best handles for spades, shovels, scythes, forks, hammers, hoes, rakes, reaping hooks and hop poles. Barrel-makers or coopers made hoops for casks from ash, while it was also common in vernacular chair-making. Ash leaves are palatable and nutritious to animals: in many parts of Europe, the dried leaves are still fed to livestock in winter.

Ash was formerly one of the most widely used medicinal

trees in Europe: its diuretic, laxative and anti-rheumatic properties made it commonplace in cures. Sailors carried crosses of ash for protection at sea, and there was a widespread belief well into the nineteenth century that ash trees could cure warts. Ronald Hutton, my old history tutor and an authority on pagan Britain, has noted that ash features more frequently in British folklore and superstition than any other tree species. Since at least Roman times, ash leaves have been infused in water with yeast and other ingredients to make a mildly alcoholic drink called *frenette*. It is still made and drunk in a few rural parts of France and Belgium.

Ash has been used to make paddles for at least 6,000 years. The Norwegian explorer Roald Amundsen had sledges constructed from ash on his successful expedition to the South Pole in 1911. The finest polar sledges are made from ash even now. Ash was exhaustively used in the manufacture of sporting goods: hockey sticks, hurley sticks, polo sticks, tennis rackets, squash rackets, badminton rackets, kites, parallel bars, cricket stumps, skis, snowshoes, toboggans, snooker cues and baseball bats. Actually, baseball bats in the USA are made from American white ash (*Fraxinus Americana*) rather than common ash, but the two species are anatomically very similar: even under a microscope, it is hard to tell between them.

Ash has contributed significantly to keeping man on the move since the dawn of civilization. For at least 4,000 years, the rims of wooden wheels have been made from ash. Before steel, the vast majority of carts, chariots and carriages also had axles and shafts made of ash. Early ancestors of the bicycle were made from ash. Coaches and then car bodies were built around ash frames. Ash was extensively used in boat-frame building and even in the manufacture of aircraft.

In military history, ash has been of equally paramount importance: it made excellent bows, spears and pike shafts. In Homer's epic *Iliad*, Achilles' spear was made of ash. It was the first choice of timber for the production of lances in the Roman Army. The black squalls of bodkin-tipped arrows that fell out of the sky and wreaked havoc among the French knights during the great battles of the Hundred Years War like Crécy and Agincourt, were commonly made of ash. The best wooden arrows are still made with ash shafts today.

John Evelyn, the eminent seventeenth-century diarist and author of one of the earliest treatises on forestry in the English language, published 350 years ago – *Sylva, or a Discourse of Forest-Trees, and the Propagation of Timber in His Majesties Dominions* – was emphatic about the importance of ash: 'In planting a whole wood of several kinds of trees, every third set at least should be ash.' Henry John Elwes, botanist, forester and co-author of a monumental work of scholarship, *The Trees of Great Britain and Ireland*, published in eight volumes between 1906 and 1913, considered ash to be the most economically viable of all British timber trees. William Cobbett, the great politicking farmer and campaigning journalist of the early nineteenth century, wrote: 'We have no tree of such various and extensive use as the Ash . . . It therefore demands our particular attention; and from me, that attention it shall have.'

Beyond a handful of experts, though, ash has never attracted the widespread acclaim it deserves: it has never drawn headlines, plaudits and the attention of poets in the same way oak has, for example. It was never the timber of kings; it was never used to make stately furniture, build vaulted cathedrals or construct Her Majesty's ships. Yet, in considering the innumerable and important historical uses, I began to wonder if ash might be the tree with which man has been most intimate over the ages. You could argue that the maintenance of a continuous supply of ash has been a strategic necessity, a foundation of domestic life and a concomitance to the promotion of mankind across Europe from prehistory almost until the present.

Out of curiosity, I began to ask more and more people what they knew about the ash. I questioned woodmen, farmers, housewives, publicans, the postman, relatives, lawyers, plumbers and total strangers I fell into conversation with on trains. A tiny minority of the vox populi I canvassed could name more than five historical uses. A handful recalled the tennis rackets, partly made of ash, which they held in their youth. The farmers all mentioned tool handles. The overwhelming majority of people I asked, though, could name only one use for ash – firewood. Ash makes excellent firewood – but really, is that it? Ash is one of the greatest gifts with which nature has endowed man in the temperate regions of the planet over the course of human history, yet it is reduced in our minds today to a material you burn. How could something so integral to our daily lives for so long, be forgotten so quickly?

I decided the best way to learn more about the ash tree was to fell one. Once the idea had germinated in my mind, it grew quickly. I would find the tree in a wood close to my home. It would be milled at my local sawmill. The best timber would be distributed to artisans and makers, to be converted into artefacts and products. I could get a writer's desk and a table made. I would turn some of the less valuable timber into panelling for my office and worktops for my kitchen. There would be chopping boards, bowls, the rims or 'felloes' of wooden wheels, spatulas, arrow shafts, catapults, tent pegs, coat racks, laths for coracles and a paddle. I could saw the larger branches up for firewood and kindling and use the smaller branches to make charcoal. I could even smoke food with the sawdust. The brash and some of the branches would be left behind on the woodland floor, to slowly rot away and eventually return to the earth as humus. Every part of my ash tree would be used: a zero-waste policy would fence the project – to exalt the worth of a single tree. How many different uses could I get from one tree, I wondered – ten, twenty, thirty, more?

No tree grows in anticipation of being felled, sawn, planked, planed, turned, sanded, drilled, moulded, routed and burned. In considering the legion applications of ash timber, though, you could be forgiven for thinking nature actually designed it to satisfy the diverse needs of human beings. As my idea formed, I started to read about the distinct properties of *Fraxinus excelsior*. At first, I found the mechanical or 'strength properties' of wood to be an impenetrable subject. Woodworking is far from being a numerically exact science: when we use timber, we depend on judgement and intuition as much as on engineering principles. I rang an acquaintance of mine, Jez Ralph, who has a company advising businesses on the properties of timber: 'Wood is an incredibly complicated material. Curiously, we're only just beginning to work this out now,' he said.

It struck me that we are still trying to get to the end of a ball of thread that Mesolithic carpenters had begun to unravel, 6,000 years ago. They were among the first to appreciate the physical characteristics inherent in different species of wood, and to employ them in producing a variety of functional wares. I wanted to look closely at the most important mechanical properties of ash – cellular structure, density, cleavability, elasticity, speed of growth, plasticity and something called 'toughness' – with reference to the key artefacts and products I commissioned.

The simple story of one tree would be set in the present, but be about the past – about the ancient accord between man and ash. It might also stand as a work of advocacy for the future, I thought. We need to recalibrate our destructive impulse with respect to nature, with our needs. I wanted to make a case for the continued and better use of the ash tree, as a sustainable resource. I also wanted to highlight something our ancestors implicitly understood – that the pleasure we take from things made from natural materials is an extension of the pleasure we take from nature itself.

My idea was beginning to take root. Boyishly, I gushed it out to my wife one evening. She looked unimpressed. Her eyebrows arched. 'Do you know a wheelwright?' she said. 'Do you know a toboggan-maker or even a bowl-turner? Do they still exist? This is the beginning of the twenty-first century, not the middle of the fifteenth. And don't you need to know a great deal about timber? I can see a large pile of very expensive firewood at the end of this venture. Perhaps there'll be enough wood left over to make the coffin you're going to bury yourself in.'

I decided not to mention the idea again. Nor did I say she had hit on one thing I would not be making from my ash: elm was traditionally used for coffins. I set off quietly at dawn the following morning with the dogs, to search for my tree.

It was an Elizabethan winter. The countryside was clamped by cold. The north-facing glacial cirques, scarps and ridges that make up the distinctive skyline of the Black Mountains looked Alpine. On the lanes, great gargoyles of snow clung to the sod banks and the hawthorn hedges. The cold had come early and swiftly, sweeping out of the north, deadening the land. The water pipes in the garden froze overnight, the songbirds disappeared and the earth turned to iron. The snow came next. It fell in big flakes at night, without noise, transforming the landscape. Next day, the fields looked like tundra. The trees had suddenly grown old.

What my wife said was true: I didn't know much about timber, but I did know roughly what tree I was looking for – an ash with a clean, straight stem or trunk that I could saw into planks of varying thicknesses and take to artisans. I also wanted a tree with a large canopy, to give me plenty of wood to work with. No tree in my own, small woodland met these criteria so I started my search in Strawberry Cottage Wood, which I help manage as part of a community woodland group. 'I don't think you'll find your tree in there,' said Jo Binns, the owner and a friend, as he was putting out feed for his sheep. He was right. Trees fight for a share of light and for nourishment: every twist in the trunk and every buttress is a show of aggression and defence. In the absence of man's intervention over several decades, the big ash in Strawberry Cottage Wood had arched, bowed and bent to gain the light. There wasn't a single, straight tree of good girth. Jo suggested I try Mark Morgan, another local farmer with a wood exclusively of ash.

It was a beautiful wood, high up on a steep hillside bordering a ridge of heather moorland in the Llanthony Valley. The trees were planted, orderly, straight and in the freezing mist, watchful. However, they were too young for my purposes. Mark, who I knew well from our collaborations on stage in the local pantomime, smiled wryly and said: 'You've saved yourself a hell of a job getting a stick down off that hillside.' He, too, was right. I wasn't just looking for the ideal ash tree; I needed a tree I could easily get to the side of the road and onto a lorry, to transport to the sawmill.

Back at home, beside my wood-burning stove, I rang all the farmers, sawmill managers, woodland owners and tree surgeons that I knew. I cold-called forestry management companies and estate managers. Some sucked their teeth and said that no one wanted good ash any more. Others humoured me. A few were helpful. The list of woodlands I was to visit in the hope of finding my ash tree grew longer as the winter strengthened.

One of the delightful curiosities of Britain is that every wood has its own name, like the villages and the great houses they are often moored to. 'I excite myself by learning the names of the woods on the Ordnance Map,' E. M. Forster wrote. Many of these names are routine: they recur across the country like patterns on an Arabic carpet – Long Wood, Park Wood, Brickyard Wood, Tanhouse Wood, Collier's Wood and Kiln Wood to name a few – and they contribute to the land's innate peace. Others read like incantations – Wasing Wood, Ragget's Wood, Mornington Coppy, Maerdy Dingle, Booby Dingle, Duck's Copse, Leigh Furzes, Ravenshot Wood, Shute Copse, Lotley Brakes, Ogbeare Wood, Trengayor Copse, Penwood and Lickham Bottom are just a few names I have come across looking at Ordnance Survey maps of Britain.

In the evenings, I pored over Google maps as well as my faded OS maps, trying to locate all the woods on my list. Each day, I set off with a flask of coffee, a tape measure, a notebook and my two spaniels. I roamed through Court Wood, Upper Wood, Lower Wood, Coed Mawr (Welsh for 'big wood'), and Wern Fawr Wood. Some days I walked through mist and the trees appeared huge. On other days, after a fall of fresh snow, the silence was magical. Occasionally, I even forgot what I was looking for: as with a long journey, the search sometimes outgrew its motives. Merely being in the woods was sufficient. Invariably, I came away buoyant after a few hours of solitary searching.

'You do realize time is against you,' Will Bullough, the local sawmill owner, told me. Several weeks had passed since we first spoke about the project. Ash, like nearly all hardwood trees, should be felled in winter. There are several reasons for this: winter-felled ash dries better; when the sap rises in ash in spring, it can colour the wood, devaluing the timber; in summer, the foliage in a tree's crown adds signifi-cant weight, increasing the risk of splits or shakes in the trunk as it falls, which can again reduce the volume and value of useful timber; finally ash, like oak, should not be felled in leaf because the sapwood is then more prone to attack from wood-boring insects. The long, cold winter, Will explained, would bank me a bit more time, but I shouldn't dither.

I had already seen several good trees, yet they were all without merit in at least one aspect. Some were straight and free of side branches, but too small; others were too old and visibly rotting from the inside out; some were inaccessible; a few were straight, save for a slight curve halfway up the trunk. My notebook was filling up with these 'not quite what I'm looking for' trees. But I wasn't panicking yet. After the con-versation with Will, though, there was a new urgency in my efforts.

In mid-February, Mark Potter, the director of a local for-estry and woodland management company, sent me an email. I had told him about the project a fortnight earlier. His email read: 'A few ashes encountered today. Are any of these candidates?' Attached were five photos: two were of ash trees in hedgerows, with short, twisted trunks; another tree had forked very low down, most likely because of frost damage early in its life – also no good to me; the last two photos were of a stand of ash at the corner of a wood. I rang Mark immediately.

Under leaden skies, we drove along the river Monnow to the Kentchurch Court estate in Herefordshire where the Scudamore family have lived since the eleventh century. Ralph de Scudemer, a stonemason from Normandy, originally came to the nearby village of Ewyas Harold to help build a stone keep for Edward the Confessor, around 1040. There were some 900 acres of woodland on the estate, much of it semi-natural ancient woodland, Mark explained. He managed it for timber, for shooting and for biodiversity. There was a huge amount of oak woodland, much of it planted when the Royal Navy was still making ships from oak, plus some mixed conifer and broad-leaf woodland. There was little mature ash. There were, however, a few trees not far from the main house, in a wood clear-felled and replanted after the First World War.

A grey, velvet pall hung over the wood. There were a dozen ash trees together, like a family, near a brook. The bark on all of them had fissured. They were mainly straight. One had the faint, graceful, feminine sweep so distinctive of ash, like a slim-hipped femme fatale in a floor-length cocktail dress. The crowns were tight, because the trees were close together. One or two of them looked near perfect. They were just too small, though. I wondered if I was now being too finicky.

'No,' Mark said generously. 'It's important you find the right tree.' Back in the car with the Ordnance Survey map on the dashboard, he showed me three other woods on the far side of the estate – Gwern-Snell, Benarth Longwood and Callow Hill Wood. 'That's good ash country. Perhaps you'll find your tree there,' he said.

My spaniels were reluctant to get out of the Land Rover when we got to Callow Hill Wood, late in the day. The wood covers a corrugation of land between the Dulas Brook and the river Dore, beside the village of Ewyas Harold with its ruined castle, five miles east of the Black Mountains. I estimated the size of the wood from the map at 12 to 15 acres and set off across the field to the southern corner. A large, forked ash with two five-metre trunks and a big crown towered over the gate – a good sign, I thought. I followed an old, sunken path from the gate into the heart of the wood. There were plots of wild cherry, areas of hazel coppice with oak standards and sections of ash coppice. Where several acres of conifers had been felled a few years ago on the northern boundary, thousands of wispy ash had self-seeded. Clearly, it was good ash-growing soil. Walking back over the brow of the hill, I passed several old charcoal-burning platforms and what I assumed was an old woodland sawpit. Dropping down the slope facing the village, I hit a seam of mature ash.

I got my tape measure out at the first tree I came to: measuring the circumference of a healthy tree at 130 centimetres above the ground and dividing the figure by 1.2 gives you a very rough estimate of the tree's age. The tree was around sixty years old. There were lots of ash, all similarly sized, among oak and cherry. I wound my way up and down the slope, scanning each tree. After fifteen minutes, as the half-light of a cussed day was thinning, I was rewarded. There it was – a mighty ash. The moment I looked up at it, I felt certain I had stood there before.

'No signs of rot or degradation and good, clean bark in the recesses between the toes,' said Mark Potter. He took a step back, looked up again and walked around the tree, out of sight. 'Good roundness. No cat's paws or other signs of rot on the stem. A good, straight, clean stem, 6 or 7 metres in length. A fair bit of volume in the crown, with good multi-structured wood. The broken branches look like they have healed well. No obvious defects. The oak trees on either side will readily fill the gap that felling the tree would create in the canopy. I think it's a good choice,' he concluded, pulling a tape measure from his pocket.

At 130 centimetres above ground, the circumference of the tree was 190 centimetres (75 inches), making the diameter 60 centimetres (23.87 inches). Using the rule of thumb calculation, this made the tree around 160 years old. Mark thought it was more like 130 to 140 years old. We walked up the bank to get a better look. All the other ash trees in the same part of the wood were around sixty years old, Mark thought, and probably planted or self-seeded after the Second World War, when many of the trees in Callow Hill Wood were felled. For some reason my tree – I was already calling it 'my tree' – had been left standing. It was hard to know why. Perhaps the woodland manager had left it as a source of ash seeds, for self-propagation. Perhaps the felling crew had run out of time before they took an axe to it. Whatever the reason, it was my good fortune.

The tree was 50 metres from the edge of the wood, on a gentle slope. Mark thought it could be felled without damaging any neighbouring trees, down the hill. Extracting the stem and the largest boughs through the fence and across the field to the side of the road would be straightforward.

Vivid green moss grew over several of the splayed toes at the base of the tree. The main stem, embellished in a patchwork of lichen and ivy, was equally thick from top to bottom, forming an almost perfect cylinder. Without a scientific device to measure the height of the main stem, I used the old manual method: holding a stick out in front of me with a straight arm, I retreated slowly until the stick and the stem appeared to be the same height; keeping my arm straight, I turned the stick sideways, marked the point where the top of the stick met the ground, at the base of a hazel stool; finally, I paced out the distance from the base of my tree to the hazel – 7 metres.

Using my phone, I calculated the volume: there was nearly 2 cubic metres of timber in the stem alone. Above the main fork, the point at which the trunk first split into two boughs, there was at least that volume of timber again. The two main boughs continued the great upward thrust of the tree in a 'V' shape. They forked again and again, tapering to a scribble of twigs upturned at their ends 30 metres above, like extravagant eyelashes. Despite the size, there was great balance and even lightness in the form of the tree.

I tried to imagine the tree as products and artefacts. It was hard. I could see some of the thinner branches stacked in piles, ready to be loaded into the community woodland group charcoal kiln; I envisaged swinging a maul into a round of ash and carrying an armful of split logs through my house to the wood-burner. I identified a couple of forks that might make catapults. I could even picture an oblong stave of ash being turned into an axe handle. That's where my imagination failed, though.

Which bit of the tree might become a paddle? Where might

the surface of my desk come from? What section would make good arrows? Which bit of timber would make the best wooden bowls? I realized how little I knew. At the same time I understood that this didn't matter: I would be helped through every step of the journey by craftsmen who did know, people who provide the continuity in human sensibility for this remarkable material. For now, it was enough to know that I had found my tree – a beautiful ash tree, the tree I would come to know better than any other, the tree that would be part of the rest of my life.

CHAPTER I

Ashes to Ashes

'[Ash] is (of all other) the sweetest of our
forest-fuelling, and the fittest for ladies chambers.'

John Evelyn,
Sylva, or a Discourse of Forest-Trees . . .

Between finding my tree and felling it, I spent a lot of time
in Callow Hill Wood. The archaeology department of the
local council sent me the report of a survey they had done on
the wood a decade ago, which informed my ramblings. The
reddish, well-drained, coarse and loamy soil sits on a bed of
hard sandstone, shale and limestone. There is evidence of
a single sawpit and several charcoal-burning pits, suggesting
the woodland was historically managed predominantly as
coppice, for the production of charcoal, once an important
rural industry. There are small quarries, probably for the
extraction of limestone, and Holloways. More interesting are
the remains of two earthworks set at right angles, running
downhill from the centre of the wood and thought to be
musketry trenches, dug to provide 'enfilading fire' across the
valley during the English Civil War. The first local skirmish
of that cataclysmic event in British history took place in Ewyas
Harold in 1642. The archaeological report concludes that
Callow Hill was probably not covered in woodland during

the Civil War, but very likely became woodland soon after that.

On one day, under the expert guidance of Ed Morell, a friend, tree surgeon and climbing instructor, I scaled my ash and sat in the canopy, high above the woodland floor. I wanted to see if the tree's form itself would reveal any insights into the best use I could make of the timber. Tree climbing is also, of course, great fun: like riding a bicycle downhill, it reminds us of childhood. I got more than I bargained for with Ed, though.

'When you're up in the canopy and the adrenaline is flowing, there is a heightened sense of awareness and at that point, a greater affinity with the tree,' Ed said, while we were getting into our harnesses on the ground. Sixty foot up, I was consumed by fear rather than a sense of affinity. I sat on a branch and watched Ed clamber, run, skate and spring through the canopy like a chimpanzee. Sometimes he landed on branches no larger than 3 inches in diameter; they swished and swayed under his weight, setting the outermost twigs of the canopy clattering into each other. He was illustrating the high strength and the flexibility of ash, but he was also having a great time. Ed estimated the height of my tree at 30 metres. The canopy, 15 metres wide at its greatest spread, had clearly grown without hindrance from neighbouring trees. It was a fine tree. I felt the first twinge of anxiety about felling it.

We spent most of the afternoon in the canopy. It was like being in a trance. Time passed so gently. When we lowered ourselves back to the ground in the weakening light, Ed said: 'It's as if you're in stasis up there. Coming back to earth all the senses kick in. It's like being born again.'

A few days later, I camped under the tree on a half moon of flat ground that was probably once a charcoal-burning pit. As night fell, I thought of the soldiers dug into their trenches further up the hill during the Civil War, preparing to 'sheathe their swords in [their countrymen's] bowels', as one contemporary chronicler put it. I thought of the charcoal-makers who camped in the woods all summer, and the woodmen from the village who would have known every coppice stool and tree. I lay in my sleeping bag under the bivvy, next to the dogs and the fire, listening to the wind in the boughs – roaring and bellowing like the voice of the Green Man. 'Inspiration', according to Robert Graves in *The White Goddess*, can be found in the 'act of listening to the wind . . . in a sacred grove'. As I fell asleep, I felt the gentle, irresistible invasion of the enchanted wood fill my last thoughts.

When I woke, the wind had dropped and the fire was out. A blanket of frost surrounded the camp. I made tea and sat on one of the roots of my tree. Ash is a deeply rooting tree, especially in mixed stands where there is competition from shallow-rooting species, and can penetrate over 6 feet into loamy, forest soils.

I thought again about felling the tree. There is a dilemma between the pleasure a tree gives while growing, and excitement at the prospect of what it might be converted into once it has been felled. 'I like to think of the tree itself: first the close, dry sensation of being wood; then the grinding of the storm; then the slow, delicious ooze of sap,' Virginia Woolf wrote in her short story, 'The Mark on the Wall'. She goes on to describe the death of the tree, concluding: 'Even so, life isn't done with;

there are a million patient, watchful lives still for a tree, all over the world, in bedrooms, in ships, on the pavement, lining rooms, where men and women sit after tea, smoking cigarettes. It is full of peaceful thoughts, happy thoughts, this tree.'

I studied the main stem. At over one hundred years old, it was a good age for an ash. Would it be better, I wondered, to leave the tree to rot and slowly crumble away, or to convert it and immortalize it as artefacts? I felt confident that felling the tree would be good for the integrity and stability of the biotic community in Callow Hill Wood. What about the spirit of the tree, though?

Across the world, people have perceived the woods and forests to be full of spirits. In India, sacred groves are thought to be full of Shakti, the uncontrollable forces of life and agents of change. In Japanese culture, folk tales are thick with imaginary creatures and spirits that roam the forests. In the Amazon rainforest, indigenous people sense spirits everywhere. The existence of a wild man of the woods, who knew the secrets of nature, was a widespread folk belief across Europe into the modern era. In *The Wind in the Willows* by Kenneth Grahame, Mr Mole is scared by the hidden eyes in the dark wood. Foresters and woodmen have continually sought to placate the spirit of trees before felling them. During the T'ang dynasty (AD c.618–907), arguably the high point of Chinese civilization, woodmen bowed to the trees and offered a promise to use the timber well, before they felled them, in obedience to the Taoist philosophy concerning the continuity in the relationship between humans and all species. The Maoris in New Zealand traditionally held a ceremony before felling a kauri tree. In parts of Germany, it was conventional to ask the permission of a tree before felling it, well into the twentieth century.

I, too, asked permission of my ash tree. In truth, I felt a bit ridiculous. But as an expression of my belief that we are bound to nature, even if we cannot see and feel it, I finished my tea, stood to attention, surveyed the tree from top to bottom and bowed. When I spoke – to ask permission and to make my promise to use the entire tree and use it well – the dogs thought I was talking to someone. They went bounding off through the wood, barking.

Felling a tree was possibly the original deed of appropriation of the natural earth by early mankind in Europe. Thousands of years ago, perhaps as he first became conscious of who he was, man lifted a heavy flint tool and struck at the base of a tree. He may have wanted the tree for shelter and fuel, or possibly to make a bridge over a river or a path through a bog, to cross into a new part of the landscape. He probably swung tentatively at first, for he saw the resemblance of his own life to that of a tree and he feared the forest, which was old then, but eventually the tree crashed to the floor, and the first act in the slow possession of the land by its people was complete.

Initially, I wanted to fell my tree with an axe. Matt Plumb, a tree surgeon who drinks in my local pub, talked me out of it. He explained that felling by axe necessarily sacrifices a large piece of the butt, the thick end of the trunk and often the most valuable part of a tree. Matt is a rare thing: he is a lumberjack and a poet. During our conversation, he told me he'd recently finished a poem about the ash tree, entitled 'Yggdrasil'.

On the shores of the Baltic Sea and deep within the great forests of northern Europe, the World Tree of Norse myth-ology, the 'greatest and best of all trees', was called Askur Yggdrasil and it was an ash tree. Yggdrasil was at the centre of the world, the Axis Mundi, the spine of the universe: with its branches and roots, it bound heaven, earth and hell together. Under its canopy, the gods held their councils. It was the tree of life, knowledge, time and space – the tree that Odin, the supreme god and creator, used to carve out the first man and woman. The belief that mankind originated from an ash tree was common to several ancient, northern European cultures. In fact, you could make a good case that ash figures more highly in European mythology than any other tree species, even oak. Richard Wagner, the composer and great collector of books on Teutonic folklore and mythology, used the sym-bolism of the World Ash Tree in his immense *Ring of the Nibelung* opera cycle.

I was so surprised to be discussing Yggdrasil in my local pub, I immediately hired Matt and his colleagues to fell my tree. The team comprised Oli, Pete, his son Jo and the lumberjack-poet himself. There was still snow on the ground the day we met in Callow Hill Wood, but the sky was diamond-bright and the air rinsed clean.

'All right, handsome?' Matt said, standing beneath my ash. I assumed this was his abbreviated homage to the tree. Then the lads were off. Pete began cutting down the young hazel that would be crushed by the stem of my ash as it fell. Oli and Matt were quickly up in the canopy on ropes with chainsaws, stripping the tree back to its basic structure, dropping the smaller branches and brash onto the floor. Jo and I collected the brash, creating a bed to cushion the fall of the main stem. Oli and Matt then felled the bigger branches in sections, to prevent damage to the canopies of the neighbouring oak trees. With a series of thumps, the smaller pieces of branch wood hit the woodland floor. The biggest branches were lowered out of the sky on ropes, to prevent damage to the timber. It was exciting to watch them work: they all knew their own role but they were also aware of what the others were doing at all times. I instinctively knew I was in good hands, on this pivotal day in my venture.

After a couple of hours, the entire crown had been dismantled, revealing a large piece of sky. The tree had been cut back to the first major fork: all that remained standing was the main trunk. It was perfectly straight, cylindrical, honest and somehow proud. Admiring it, Pete said: 'Aye, decent stick that.'

We stopped for lunch, using the branches as benches – the first use of my tree, I thought. The smell of freshly cut ash hung about us. We tidied up the last of the branch wood and then Oli hauled his big chainsaw to life. Making a large tree fall not just where you want it but precisely when you want it, requires great experience and skill. He made the 'sink cut' near the base of the tree, in the direction it would fall – down the slope, towards the edge of the wood. Next, he 'dressed the tree', cutting off sections of the roots where they flared from the base and disappeared into the ground. Then, cautiously at first, feeling his way into the tree, Oli began the 'felling cut'.

I stood back and watched, reflecting on the lifespan of the tree as the cutting teeth of the chain began to rip through the wood. As the saw touched the tree, it was slicing through the growth of 2014 and into 2013. Within a few seconds, the blade was whirring through 2000 and the millennium, when beacon fires burned on the hilltops nearby and fireworks filled the night sky above the village. Suddenly, we were in 1976 – a tough summer for big ash trees that like water – then the great winter of 1963, when polar winds scraped the bare trees for weeks on end.

Oli paused for a moment. He peered around the butt, to check the position of the blade tip and the angle of the cut. Satisfied, he began sawing again. Sawdust from the 1950s spewed in a jet from the bottom of the blade. Soon, Oli was cutting through 1947 – another legendary winter: snow lay on the ground for eight weeks during a fuel crisis, leading to a spike in the demand for firewood. Then it was the Second World War, a time of almost unprecedented pressure on Europe's timber resource: 500,000 acres of woodland were chopped down across Britain in just six years. Between the wars, a quarter of Callow Hill Wood was felled, cleared and replanted with conifers, to provide pit props for the mines in South Wales. Oli paused again, to check the symmetry of the cut and to catch his breath.

In the final phase, the cutting teeth carved out another drought year, 1919, when the Forestry Commission was established; then on through the dark years of the First World War when the nation's woodlands were severely depleted, past the death of Queen Victoria in 1901 to the dawn of the twentieth century. As the chainsaw kissed the pith or heart of the tree, around 1885, the bicycle and the motor car were being invented.

Oli looked up and studied the stem. He squared the cut off with the chainsaw, on the opposite side. The saw fell silent. We were ready. Pete and Jo were in position down the slope, holding a rope fixed to the top of the trunk. With a sledge-hammer, I drove two steel wedges into the gap where the saw had been. On the third strike, the thin 'hinge' that Oli had left holding the tree upright began to crack. There was a pier-cing creak. With a thump that echoed through the entire wood, my tree landed on the bed of brash. Over a century of steady growth was ended in a moment.

The wind makes music in the woods, but the tune changes with the seasons.

Spring had unmistakably arrived in Callow Hill Wood when I returned. Most of the trees were in leaf. Inside the gate, between a large ash and a stand of wild cherry trees, I stood still, closed my eyes and listened. In Thomas Hardy's *The Woodlanders*, Giles Winterborne could distinguish species of trees at a distance, simply from 'the quality of the wind's mur-mur through a bough'. It is a wonderful thought – that a man's intimacy with trees can be so sensuous. It speaks of a former epoch, when the forest figured highly in the lives of the major-ity of European people. Even listening intently, I could make no distinction between the notes from the canopies of the different species. It was all one soft washing sound of water pouring through shingle.

In the glade where my tree had stood, I began dragging the boughs that I would convert into firewood down the slope to the edge of the wood, one by one. On a makeshift sawhorse, I cut the branches with a chainsaw into 4-foot lengths and threw them over the fence into the field. When my back began to ache, I drove my Land Rover around and filled the trailer.

The brash, some of the smaller-diameter branch wood and several of the larger logs would stay where they fell, on the woodland floor. Throughout its life, my ash tree had played a part in the natural community of Callow Hill Wood, yet it had another function in death. Rotting or decaying wood is a hugely important part of the ecology of woodlands. As the structure and composition of deadwood changes over decades of gentle decay, it provides sanctuary and sustenance to an evolving legion of wildlife species: insects, fungi, mosses, lichens, invertebrates and small mammals. In fact, some species can only live in deadwood. The rule of thumb, at least for conservation-minded woodmen, is to leave one quarter of a tree for the benefit of the woodland, where it will rot along with the fallen leaves and eventually return to the earth as humus. Decades from now, that humus will encourage ash seeds to become saplings, in the continual process of death and renewal that is a fundamental facet of the woodland ecosystem.

At home, I unloaded the trailer beside my woodshed. My children scattered at the sound of the Land Rover, knowing they would be collared to help, while my wife pretended to be on the phone through the window. When she emerged from the house with a cup of coffee, I was shouldering the last of the boughs off the trailer onto the pile. 'Look at my little Neanderthal man,' she said, 'gathering fuel to keep the tribe warm over winter.'

Learning to control fire was a major turning point in human evolution. For us, providing fuel has been the primary function of trees, in terms of volume, ever since. Our primate species, *Homo sapiens*, has been using fire to stay warm, scare predators and cook food to make it more digestible for around 200,000 years. Nearly half the world's population still cooks on wood today.

In Europe, wood remained the main source of energy for the majority of people until the Industrial Revolution. During the Middle Ages, fuel in the form of logs, faggots (bundles of sticks bound together) and charcoal came from the underwood of smaller trees and coppice growth, usually after the woodworking artisans had taken their pick. In Britain during Tudor and Stuart times, around 1500 to 1700, firewood prices rose dramatically, for several reasons. Chimneys became more common and the expanding demand for timber as a building material, and charcoal for iron manufacturing and the production of pottery and glass, placed great demands on our woodlands. An increase in the cultivation and grazing of land, significantly for the wool trade, meant that woodlands were simply stripped of trees and turned into fields, further reducing the resource. Also, at this time, northern Europe was subject to a period of cooler weather known as the 'Little Ice Age', characterized by heavy spring and autumnal rains, big storms and critically, cycles of severe winters. During the mid-sixteenth century, as a result, Britain experienced its first energy crisis, as the price of firewood spiked. In some regions, the price was so high and the shortage so severe that families had no fire in the hearth – the same hearth where wood had been burned without a thought for thousands of years. By the end of the sixteenth century, coal was being used as an alternative heating fuel in urban areas: it was the first widespread use of a non-renewable fuel.

At the time of the Industrial Revolution, the infrastructure to distribute new forms of energy like gas was built into cities, promoting domestic convenience, while the railways brought cheap coal to the countryside. In 1859, oil was first drilled for in Titusville, Pennsylvania, providing an apparently plentiful energy source to replace coal. The advent of central heating and successive fashions for oil, natural gas, propane and atomic energy meant wood, a more labour-intensive fuel for the user, was quietly forgotten.

In the last two decades, wood as fuel has made a small comeback in industrialized nations. The prices of oil and natural gas have reached a point where wood has become an economically viable domestic heat source again for some. Wood is, of course, also a renewable resource, providing we burn it at sustainable levels. It is the only form of do-it-yourself fuel – a matter of importance to many, including myself, who wish to limit their exposure to the bewildering forces of the global economy by bringing the provenance of things closer to home.

I have three wood-burning stoves: one in the main room in the house; one in the converted byre next to the house; the third is in my office, a small cabin in the woods below the house. The first free-standing, cast-iron stove was designed in 1742, by Benjamin Franklin, the American statesman and polymath who once said 'be frugal and free'. Stoves are much more efficient than open fires because the draught of air going into the stove and up the chimney can be controlled. Throughout the nineteenth century, cast-iron stoves became hugely popular. Recently, renewed interest in wood fuel has prompted the development of a new generation of stoves, which burn wood even more efficiently and cleanly. Along with 96 per cent of British homes, we have central heating in the house, fired by oil. The wood-burning stove there is used to supplement the heating system through the coldest part of winter, but it replaces the oil in spring and autumn. In the byre and the cabin, wood is the sole heat source.

My woodland at home is small. There is a mix of oak, alder, beech, birch, holly, hazel, lime, hawthorn, maple, wych elm, the odd sweet chestnut and a lot of ash. When I began working in the wood, firewood started to pile up. I slipped quietly into the annual cycle of cutting back trees in winter, splitting and stacking wood in spring, leaving it to season through the summer, transferring it to the woodshed in autumn, and burning it to keep the tribe warm the following winter, or the winter after that. This cycle is now a cardinal component of my existence. It makes me part of an ancient tradition and gives me a role in the landscape. I often wonder how I ever knew domestic contentment without it.

I walk through my wood most days, either with the dogs to get to the common land beyond, or to my office. In spring, the trees are full of bird banter. In summer, rods of sunlight fall through the canopy. Sometimes, I wonder fancifully if the sound of the breeze in the trees is a sigh of contentment, like my spaniels settling down beside the fire in winter. Certainly, I feel I have at last taken ownership of my wood.

In providing fuel, my woodland also saves me hundreds of pounds a year – an economic value that ensures I care for it in return. I use around four to five tonnes (4,000–5,000 kg) of seasoned firewood each year. It is always a boon to supplement the supply from my own woodland, especially with ash. As John Wyatt wrote in *The Shining Levels*, his account of working as a forester in the Lake District during the 1950s, ash is 'the darling of wood burners.'

It is hard to be sure when ash first got its reputation as a pre-eminent firewood species. There are many anonymous, often regional firewood rhymes from different countries that attest to it, but they are largely undated. In Britain, John Evelyn extolled the virtues of ash as fuel in the seventeenth century. The popular poem 'Logs to Burn', written during the British coal strike in 1926 by Honor Goodhart, concludes that ash logs are 'worth their weight in gold.' The often-quoted 'The Firewood Poem' by Celia Congreve, first published in *The Times* in 1930, reviews fifteen different species of firewood, not always accurately, and is emphatic in its conclusion:

> But ash green and ash brown
> Is fit for a queen with golden crown.

This esteem for ash as firewood partly relates to the amount of water stored in the wood when a tree is felled. All wood contains water and there are several different ways of measuring the moisture content. The most common and practical method is to take the gross weight of a green log, dry it completely in a kiln, and measure it again, which reveals the proportion that is wood and the proportion that is water. So, if a log weighing 1 kg contains 400 g of water and 600g of wood, it is said to have 40 per cent moisture content. The moisture content of different tree species when they are felled in mid-winter varies hugely. The indicative figure given for poplar wood, for example, is 65 per cent water; elm is 58 per cent; European larch is 50 per cent; oak and beech are 47 per cent (also the mean figure for all hardwood species); birch is 43 per cent and sycamore comes in at a more respectable 41 per cent. With respect to moisture content, ash is in a class of its own: freshly felled ash has a moisture content of just 33 per cent.

Of course, almost nobody burns wood when it is freshly felled and full of water. It is a poor idea for several reasons. It creates unnecessary smoke, it is a cause of air pollution and, crucially, the energy content or calorific value (the amount of heat released per unit of fuel burnt) of wet wood is much lower, because the heat produced by combustion has to evaporate all the water before the wood can actually burn, using up a large percentage of the available energy in the process. Finally, burning wet wood can deposit flammable resins like tar in the chimney and cause fires.

Most people dry wood to a practical point at which it will burn more readily and efficiently – around 20 per cent, pretty much the lowest moisture content logs will reach in northern Europe if they are stacked to dry outside. At 20 per cent moisture content, the calorific value of wood is acceptable. However, you can burn ash without drying it, if you have to, as Celia Congreve suggests. I prefer not to. I like to cut, split and store ash for a minimum of six warm, dry weeks – and I would only burn it then in the event of a critical shortage. Ideally, I like to season ash over a summer.

Ash has other qualities, however, which set it apart as firewood. Because the wood is relatively dense and contains a lot of cellulose (a carbohydrate that forms the cell walls of all plants), it burns agreeably slowly: alder, birch and sycamore, for example, burn quicker. Ash also contains a comparatively high amount of oleic acid, a flammable, unsaturated fatty acid. As ash splits easily, I tend to chop it into smaller pieces, which catch better in the fire. The smoke from green ash has a gentle fragrance, like air-dried washing; well-seasoned ash, on the other hand, burns with little smoke and it doesn't spit, both great advantages on an open hearth or a campfire. The ashes from an ash fire contain a high percentage of potash, which can be used in the garden as a good source of potassium.

Together, these characteristics have historically made a good case for ash as excellent firewood. Modern research supports that too. Tests in Scandinavia into the net calorific value of different trees at 20 per cent moisture content rank the common species, in increasing value: poplar, spruce, aspen, alder, willow, larch, maple, birch, ash, beech, oak and robinia. Ash may not be supreme solely with respect to energy content then, but when all its advantageous traits are considered together, it is very hard to argue against it (though people do). We all have our favourite firewood: this is partly prejudice and partly the poetic preferences of people adjusted to their own surroundings. In the end, all well-seasoned wood will burn, and the best fires burn on a mix of species.

When I had finished my cup of coffee, I cross-cut the ash branch wood with a chainsaw into 1-foot lengths. I was ready to start splitting. I have a friend who refers to his ash logs as 'Hollywood logs': splitting them is often effortless, like being swept away to Tinsel Town by a movie. Certainly for me, splitting rounds of ash into logs is the most physically and psychologically satisfying part of the entire firewood cycle; at the same time, trying to split sycamore, adamantine oak or dry alder with an axe can be the most tortuous part. Ash also splits well green or seasoned, while most other tree species are harder to split if they have been left to dry first. There are two main reasons for splitting firewood: to make the logs small enough to fit inside my stoves, and to increase the volume to surface area of each log, speeding up the rate at which the wood dries. I use two tools depending on the size and, to some extent, the species of timber I am splitting: a 3-lb axe and an 8-lb maul or 'splitting axe'.

Mike Abbott, one of Britain's last traditional chair-makers, works exclusively with green or unseasoned wood, using non-mechanized techniques. How wood splits or cleaves is fundamental for Mike, just as it was for generations of woodworkers involved in a host of crafts, from chair-bodging to making fence rails, via split shingles, bow-making, barrel-making and the production of billets for tool handles. Long before the invention of powered saws, green woodworkers developed the skill of cleaving, effectively a controlled version of splitting wood, in order to make best use of the foremost characteristics of the tree, and also simply to make a piece of wood roughly the right size for their various purposes. Generally, green woodworkers want high cleavability – wood that splits easily.

Mike works almost entirely with ash. On the grass outside his workshop in the rolling Herefordshire countryside, he gave me a brief cleaving demonstration before handing me a green ash log, 10 centimetres in diameter and a metre long. I took a froe, a cleaving tool with the handle at right angles to the slightly wedged, metal blade, and smacked it into the end of the log with a wooden club. I levered the handle: with a tearing sound, the log split straight down the grain, into two. I split those two pieces into four. The splits weren't perfect, but Mike assured me there was a chair rung in each piece. 'Try that with a bit of beech and it wouldn't go. At least, it wouldn't go straight,' Mike said. He talked about using 'sensitive force' to encourage the splits to run as straight as possible; about how you 'collaborate' with the wood in cleaving, and how ash cleaves well both radially (through the centre of a round piece of wood) and tangentially (perpendicular to the grain but tangential to the growth rings).

In science, cleavability, technically known as 'maximum cleavage strength', is conventionally measured in Newtons (a unit of force) per millimetre and tested for in radial and tangential directions, in both green and dry states. Low cleavability (or high resistance to splitting) is important in certain uses of wood today, because it indicates the ability of a particular

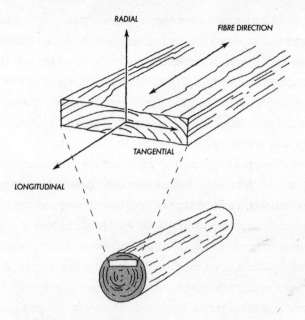

RADIAL

FIBRE DIRECTION

TANGENTIAL

LONGITUDINAL

Radial, tangential and longitudinal axes in a flatsawn board

species to hold nails and screws. Different tree species cleave in very different ways. Both density and elasticity (properties of wood considered in following chapters) have some influence on cleavability, but the form of the grain has a more pronounced effect. Species like elm, yew, holly and sycamore have interlocking grain, often the result of repeated cycles of spiral growth in the tree, and they are highly resistant to splitting. Ash, on the other hand, cleaves or splits very well. The main reason for this is that the grain in ash is commonly, and notably, straight: that is, the direction of the grain is parallel or virtually parallel to the direction the tree grows.

In the world of wood and timber, 'grain' is a confusingly

versatile term with numerous different meanings, many of which are only clarified by context or associated adjectives. In this case, 'grain' describes the alignment of the dominant cells in the wood. It can be qualified in phrases like 'across the grain', 'against the grain', 'along the grain' and 'with the grain', or with adjectives like spiral, cross, curly, close, wavy, interlocking and straight.

To fully understand what grain is, it helps to take a step back and consider what wood is and how trees grow. Wood is a composite material made up mainly of cellulose fibres in a structure of lignin (a glue-like chemical substance that binds the cellulose and makes it rigid). Complex cells form the basic unit of life and they display a high degree of self-organization. A tree increases in diameter over time by forming new woody layers between the bark and the old wood. These woody layers envelop the stem, all the living branches and the roots of the tree. In hardwood trees like ash, the layers comprise a variety of cell types with specialized functions. Two main kinds of cells dominate: xylem, in a mass of open, tubular vessels that form end to end, a bit like pipelines, and carry water, dissolved minerals, oxygen and nitrogen from the earth, via the roots, up to the leaves; and phloem (the inner bark), which comprises strings of vascular tissues that carry sugars and other metabolic products of photosynthesis down from the leaves to all the other parts of the tree. Cambium, a stem-cell tissue which forms a sheath around the tree, produces both xylem and phloem.

Trees produce new cells each year to perform two main functions: to support the crown of the tree so it can maintain its position above shorter plants in order to capture more

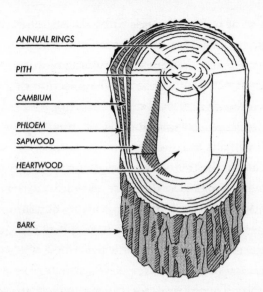

ANNUAL RINGS

PITH

CAMBIUM

PHLOEM

SAPWOOD

HEARTWOOD

BARK

sunlight, enabling photosynthesis to take place in the leaves; and to transport water and food. Since both functions are required in the direction the tree grows – upwards from the ground – most of the cells that form the xylem are oriented in that direction. Thus, if you magnify the cross section of a tree, it is a bit like looking end on at a huge bunch of straws.

The tree thickens as it gets older, to make a wider column to support the crown as it grows bigger and higher – a process called 'secondary thickening'. The cells that form the tubes of the xylem, in turn, die and give up their active role conducting water: all that is left is the cell wall, comprising cellulose stiffened with lignin. As successive new layers of xylem are formed, the old xylem becomes increasingly blocked up with mineral deposits, gums and resins, which is why the

43

heartwood of trees like ash is often darker than the active sapwood.

Under normal conditions, one new layer of wood is formed each year. When you look at the cross section of a tree cut horizontally, each new layer appears as a ring. These are commonly referred to as 'growth rings' or 'annual rings' and, as any child will tell you, if you count the number of rings, you have the age of the tree. These concentric rings vary in width from species to species: they also vary in width within an individual tree, according to the growing conditions of the particular year. (In temperate regions where ash grows, of course, the growing season is only part of the year – roughly March to October.)

In species like oak and ash, the xylem cells are relatively large and distinct: in some cases, you can see them with the naked eye. In other species, the cells can only be identified with a magnifying glass. Where there is a visible contrast within a single growth ring (as with ash), the inner or first formed layer of xylem is called 'earlywood' (or 'springwood'), and the outer layer is called 'latewood' (or 'summerwood'). The earlywood forms during the first part of the annual growing season, when growth is rapid: it comprises thin-walled, lower-density cells or vessels with larger cavities that appear lighter in colour. The latewood cells, created towards the end of the growing cycle, are smaller, thicker-walled, denser and darker. Latewood also contains a greater proportion of lignin and other wood fibres that give strength and toughness to wood. Hardwood species like ash, with a concentration of the largest pores in the earlywood, are called 'ring-porous'.

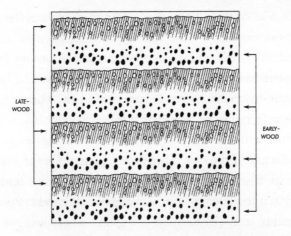

LATE-
WOOD

EARLY-
WOOD

Magnified end grain of ash, showing earlywood and latewood

Other hardwoods with an even distribution of these pores are called 'diffuse-porous.'

As the strength of wood tends to be in the cell walls rather than in the cavities, the size, number and distribution of xylem vessels (and the proportion of cell wall to cavity) are determining factors not just in the appearance but also in the uniformity of hardness of a piece of wood. Hence the greater the proportion of latewood, the greater the density and strength of a piece of wood. Ring-porous woods, then, have a weak point because the vessels, the weaker structural elements of wood, are concentrated. This is basically why ash splits or cleaves so easily.

I'm not entirely sure why I enjoy splitting firewood with an axe so much, but I am not alone in this. 'All good men love an axe,' the pioneering ecologist John Stewart Collis wrote in *The Worm Forgives the Plough*, his memoir published in 1973 about working the land during and immediately after the Second World War. Leo Tolstoy regarded axe-work as a religious discipline. George Bernard Shaw once declared it kept him sane. One obvious attraction is the sheer physical exertion: 'The wood warmed me twice, once while I was splitting them, and again when they were on the fire, so that no fuel could give out more heat,' Henry David Thoreau wrote in *Walden; or, Life in the Woods* (1854), his reflective book about life on the shores of Walden Pond in Massachusetts.

The exercise uses several muscle groups in the body, while the effort produces endorphins and adrenaline. There is also the basic pleasure of standing up and being outside, of feeling the rain on my face and an ache in my lower back, which is important if you sit at a desk for much of the day, as I do. Chopping firewood can be done in short bursts – in fact, little and often is the best way to approach a large pile – yet, as the logs mount in a stack around your chopping block, there is an obvious and pleasing sense of progress after just half an hour. If I keep at it for longer, I can fall into a trance chopping wood: it is a form of meditation, albeit with a lethal weapon. Somehow my capacity to concentrate, and strike the log precisely where I want, is heightened in this state; meanwhile the general debris of daily life gently empties from my head, leaving a void. Paradoxically, in this void, I sense I am exercising my judgement and sharpening my cognitive attentiveness, a human virtue that degenerates in many other parts of my daily life.

There is also a measure of gratification in the logs them-selves. As it's easier to make a good fire with a selection of logs, I tend to cut my wood to different sizes. The variety in shape, weight and colour is endless, and aesthetically pleasing. Each swing of the axe is like turning the page of a book; it opens a new part of the tree, and elicits a little bit more infor-mation about the tree's life: V-shaped and ellipsoid figures, curly grain, ray flecks, dimples, tight knots, loose knots, bark pockets and staining from diverse fungi might all show for the first time when a log is split open.

I love the sound that the axe makes splitting the log. This sound varies, depending on how hard you swing and the size of the log. Strike a round log, three feet in diameter, and you get a deep, heavy thunk that resonates through the chopping block, into the ground and back up your legs. Let the maul drop on a 6-inch log and it splits with a ting or a twang. These sounds vary again, from one species to another. With par-ticularly fibrous wood like hazel, for example, the initial sound is supplemented with a tearing noise. They also change accord-ing to how wet or dry the logs are. The sound of logs being split will also speak of the accuracy and skill of the woodcutter. Put the axe in the hands of an expert and you will hear an assuring symphony; set an eager debutant to the task and the woodshed will ring with a jarring cacophony. Either way, to chop your own wood is to quietly resist the mechanization of the countryside.

Yet it is the physical sincerity of the act itself – swinging a lump of steel through the air at 50mph, and bursting it into a block of wood – that I find so continuously enthralling. When

I strike a large, knotted lump of oak from near the base of a tree, and the bevel of the axe rebounds leaving only the faintest impression, the failed effort surges back through the ash handle, up my arms and into my shoulders. That is the strength of a tree that resisted the will of innumerable gales. On the other hand, when the steel axe-edge breaks the surface of an ash log and the 'cheeks' of the blade race down through the cleft in the grain like water surging between rocks, sending two white logs their separate ways, there is a sense of completeness in the act that sings through my entire body. Sometimes I find the execution of the job overwhelmingly satisfying. It has the momentary physical pleasure of timing a tennis shot perfectly, or creaming a football on the half volley. For an act of mundane, daily labour, splitting ash is without equal.

When all the ash logs were split, I stacked them on a lattice of hazel sticks, oriented to face the prevailing wind, against the uphill side of four tree trunks, either side of my office in the woods. I estimated there was half a tonne of unseasoned firewood. There was probably the same amount again still to be collected from Callow Hill Wood. The ash would be ready to burn next winter, I thought, when I would be holed up in my office writing this book.

CHAPTER 2

Hafts and Helves

'The toolmaker, called by some the master of all
trades, had first to go to the woodman for hafts and
handles cleft from pliant ash.'

H. L. Edlin

The trunk of my tree was being carried high across the yard
on a forklift truck when I arrived at the sawmill. Deftly, it was
lowered onto the metal bed of the large band saw and secured
with steel teeth called 'dogs'. Within minutes, the saw was off,
whirring into the outside slab of the log called a 'flitch'. The
smell of freshly cut ash filled the air.

This was a big day for me, a turning point in my year.
Though experts can interpret a great deal from a tree while it
is still standing in the forest, you don't really know whether
you have got any decent timber until the trunk is sawn into
planks. Of course, no one else at Whitney Sawmills was excited.
Will Bullough, the boss, poked his head around the office door,
waved and returned to his desk. Gareth Jones, the saw operator, already had a list of the different plank sizes I wanted: he
certainly wasn't waiting around for my heart to settle.

The first five planks were all 1-inch thick. As they came off
the saw, I felt a surge of excitement. The top boards were
creamy white and clean – classic ash timber. I knew they

were called 'crown boards' and valued by furniture makers, because they often have interesting grain patterns. As the saw got closer to the centre of the log, the colour of the timber began to change. In the middle of each board there was a wide stripe of darker wood sometimes called 'olive ash' or 'black heart', with a hue that varied from dark grey to laurel green. The grain here was heavily pronounced, like seams of mineral deposits in rock.

There are two principal ways of sawing timber – 'quarter-sawn' and 'plain sawn'. Will had suggested the latter. Each cut is made lengthwise, one after the other, like slicing a loaf of bread the long way. In this fashion there is less waste, the repercussions from any defects in the tree tend to be minimized, and ornate patterns arising from the annual rings are more evident. Also, because there is less handling at the sawmill, it is quicker and cheaper.

Every few minutes, Gareth sprung onto the forklift truck to move two or three sawn boards off the top of the log and onto

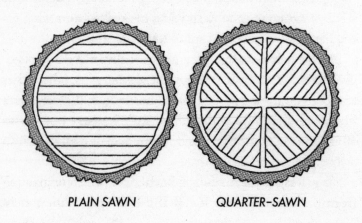

PLAIN SAWN   QUARTER-SAWN

temporary stacks in the yard. The next two boards were 1¼ inches thick, a common dimension of timber used in the manufacture of tool handles. There was a 3-inch board, part of which would go to the wheelwright to be made into the rims of wooden wheels. Next, a pair of 2-inch boards came off the log. It was happening fast. I had many questions to ask Gareth, but he was absorbed in doing the job well and speaking to him meant waiting for the right moment, dancing around the machinery and exclaiming through the wall of noise into his ear defenders.

Will strode over to inspect the timber, as the saw blade progressed through another cut. He swept the sawdust away and raised his glasses. He flicked at something with a thumbnail and lowered his face closer to the ash. He swiped dust in a couple of other places and examined the bark. My log had been dragged behind a tractor out of Callow Hill Wood, across a field and down a track, to the roadside, picking up mud and stones in the fissures of bark on the way. As stones can blunt and damage the expensive saw blades, I had spent an afternoon scrubbing the log clean with a brush and picking out stones with a penknife. Will stood back, slowly nodding his head: it was a tacit seal of approval.

Past the halfway point, the amount of olive wood decreased. Two boards were 1¾ inches, again a good size for tool handles and perhaps even a paddle from the clean, straight-grained timber near the edge of the boards. The next board was 9⁄16-inch, an irregular timber size that would be converted into arrow shafts. The last board was 1¼-inch.

There was a small amount of 'heart shake', a cleft originating from the centre of the log at the butt end. Common in over-mature hardwood trees, shake usually results from shrinkage of the heartwood due to chemical changes. Fortunately, the shake only extended for a short distance through a few of the boards. Even more importantly, there were very few 'knots' in my timber. Knots are the remains of side branches that broke off long ago and were subsequently surrounded by new wood on the trunk. Though they provide interesting, aesthetic detail for diverse woodworkers, they are also weak points in the timber and regarded as defects by the industry.

The slabs or 'flitches' from the top and the bottom of the log had more bark than wood: they would be converted into firewood. The sawdust had been extracted through pipes into a storage container: it is sold to local farmers who use it as animal bedding. In fact, the sawmill is governed by a strong environmental policy and little goes to waste. Whitney is a supplier of timber certified by the Forest Stewardship Council or FSC, the international organization promoting the responsible management of the world's forests, while Will himself is very committed to sustainable forestry and woodland management in the UK. When I had rung to tell him that the tree was felled, Will's first question was about my replanting plans.

It was the end of the shift. The machines were shutting down. Gareth went off for a mug of tea. After the screech of the saws, the silence was refreshing: it was like stepping out of a smoky room into the night air. Will emerged from his office to inspect my timber again. He stooped forward to examine the olive-coloured wood. All ash trees this age have some discolouring, he explained, and though the mechanical properties of darker wood are no different, white ash tends to sell for a higher price. Whitney Sawmills still saws a reasonable amount of home-grown ash, for a variety of end uses including flooring, fine-furniture components, parts for yurts and vintage-car restoration projects. However, Will told me, the consumption of ash in the UK is dominated by imports of white ash from the USA.

Together we shifted a few of the planks to examine the timber from the top of the log. There were fourteen boards, all 19 feet long. The taper from end to end was minimal. Freshly sawn, the white timber was beginning to turn pinkish. Will smiled brightly. 'Even though you felled it late, your ash tree has not got a lot of sap in it. That's good news,' he said, standing beside me with his hands dug deep into his back pockets. 'This is a decent tree. You've got a lot of good-quality timber here. We'll deliver it to your home in the next few days, with instructions on how to season it. I hope you have a good plan to use it well. I wonder where you're going to start. Tool handles?'

The earliest, rudimentary stone tools, invented around two and a half million years ago, had no handles. They were, however, a fundamental step forward for our distant ancestors: they were the first instruments to separate us from all other creatures and the initial step on the staircase of inventions which man has, from age to age, scaled in order to refashion his environment.

A giant leap forward in tool technology, extending the scope of the human hand to tap the potential in nature, seems to have taken place around 7,000 BC, at the beginning of the

Neolithic period. Two things happened: we learnt how to polish and sharpen the stone tool heads, which made them more efficient; around the same time, tool heads were attached to handles, also known as 'hafts' or 'helves'. These first handles were made of animal bones or wood. Having the tool head further away from the hand magnified the power of the human arm. It has been suggested that the proliferation, specialization and improvement of these tools, including axes, chisels, gouges and adzes (an edge tool with the blade set at right angles to the shaft), was significant in determining our conversion from nomadic hunters and herdsmen into settled farmers.

In Northern Europe, the greatest impediment to settlement was the forest. In a series of experiments conducted in the middle of the twentieth century, Neolithic axe heads held in the collection of the National Museum of Denmark in Copenhagen, and last sharpened some 4,000 years ago, were fitted to new ash handles (modelled on a Neolithic ash handle found in a peat bog). The tools were then set to use in the forest. Once the correct technique had been ascertained, trees were felled readily: an oak more than 1 foot in diameter came down in thirty minutes, while ⅛ of an acre (0.05 hectares) of silver birch forest was felled in four hours. Clearly, late Stone Age men and women with their flint axes had little trouble making clearings in the extensive forests that then covered large parts of the landscape, in preparation for cultivating the land.

These ground, polished and hafted tools also paved the way for wood to play a strategic role in the domestic life of Stone Age man (other than as fuel, of course). Timber for building homes, basic furniture, cooking utensils, canoes, paddles, frames for hide-covered boats and fishing nets, as well as bows, spears, sleds and skis, could be fashioned with some precision for the first time. So too could the handles for the tools themselves.

Archaeologists are cautious about dating a dramatic increase in the use of hafted tools in Europe, because of the relatively small number of contemporary wooden artefacts that have survived from Neolithic times. As wood is organic, it perishes relatively quickly when exposed to air. However, the wooden pieces that we do have, from waterlogged sites beside lakes, in bogs and occasionally on the seashore, suggest woodworkers had extensive working knowledge of the functional characteristics of different species of wood.

Though the standardization of timbers for specific applications was probably not complete until the Middle Ages in Europe, there is some consistency in the way certain tree species were used to make certain artefacts during Neolithic times: small chisel handles were produced out of poplar and willow; yew was commonly used for bows; knife handles were made from, amongst others species, yew, beech, wild cherry and elm; examples of awls, a small pointed tool for piercing holes, have been found with yew and elm hafts. The most consistent example of a single species being preferentially used for a specific tool during Neolithic times, however, is ash for axe handles. Time and again, archaeologists at wetland sites from Sweden to Slovenia via France and Switzerland have discovered axes with hafts fashioned out of common ash.

Of course, not every Neolithic axe handle was made from ash. Ötzi the Iceman, a naturally preserved body chanced upon in the Tyrolean Alps in 1991, is one of the greatest arch-aeological finds of all time. The artefacts discovered on the Iceman provide a remarkable time capsule dating from over 5,000 years ago. Eighteen different species of wood have been identified in the collection of tools he carried: the handle of his copper axe is made of yew, while the haft of his flint dagger is made out of ash. They should be the other way round.

Technologically, too, the axe continued to improve: sockets and sleeves of deer antlers were used to fix the hafts to the stone heads; hafts became jointed at one time, to reduce the chance of their breaking; through the last two millennia BC, stone was widely supplanted by bronze, copper and then iron as the material of choice for the heads, as metalworking skills improved and tools became even more specialized. Axes with iron heads, similar in size and shape to what we know today, were developed around 500 to 200 BC. By this time, the asso-ciation between ash and tool handles had cemented itself in the mind of the agricultural labourer throughout Europe.

The legacy of this is still visible in the landscape today. From the foothills of the French Pyrenees to the windswept Pennines in north-east England, and from the Åland archi-pelago in the Baltic Sea to the plains of the Po Valley in Italy, you will commonly find ash trees growing beside farms. They are not clean, straight woodland trees like mine. Often they are old and misshapen, like the spines of the farmers who cultivated them. They were, and in some instances still are, working trees that were pollarded (the ancient practice of cutting trees back above head height, on a regular cycle from an early age, and leaving them to sprout new branches from the top of the trunk) or coppiced intermittently over centuries to provide poles to be turned into implements for use on the farm: shepherd's crooks, rakes, ladders, thatching spars, rims for sifters and sieves, collars and fasteners for animals, ploughs, harrows, hoes, hop poles and hurdles were all shaped out of the easily worked ash, as were the best handles for forks, spades, shovels, scythes, reaping hooks, slashers and axes.

Ash trees served one other noteworthy function at farmsteads across Europe: the leaves were harvested to feed livestock. Until the beginning of the twentieth century, dried ash leaves, known as 'ash hay' and rich in proteins, were a familiar part of winter feed for cattle, sheep, pigs and goats. In isolated places like the Massif Central in France, this traditional way of providing fodder continues today. I have actually witnessed how nourishing sheep find ash leaves. I once felled a small ash tree in summer into a field bordering woodland: a flock of sheep devoured the leaves in minutes.

By the time humans started writing about silviculture, or the growing and cultivation of trees, ash was undisputed as the material of choice for tool handles. In *Sylva, or a Discourse of Forest-Trees, and the Propagation of Timber* . . ., published in 1664, John Evelyn wrote there is 'Nothing like it for . . . handles, stocks for tools, spade-trees, &c. In sum, the husbandman cannot be without the ash'. The ash tree was even nicknamed 'the husbandry tree', because it was so useful to people who worked the land. In 1825, William Cobbett noted in his own discourse on growing trees, *The Woodlands*: 'ash . . . contributes towards the making of tools of almost all sorts'. As Will Bullough's question to me suggested, the remarkable, ancient association between ash and handles for tools endures to this day.

'Ash is strong and flexible, as they knew thousands of years ago. It's not too heavy. It doesn't splinter. It wears smoothly. In fact, the more you use an ash handle, the kinder it is to the human hand. It's readily available and inexpensive. It's consistent. It's easy to work. Stop me if I'm banging on. Cup of tea?' John Lloyd said. Tall, with a booming voice, John is the third generation to run the family tool-handle manufacturing business, A. S. Lloyd & Son of South Wales.

While John went to put the kettle on, I opened the old hardback company brochure he'd left on the table in his office; it dated back to the middle of the twentieth century. It advertised A. S. Lloyd & Son's 'Excelsior' brand of ash wares – here were handles for hammers, hay forks, hay rakes, scythes, snaths, Welsh, Devon and Cornish shovels, navvy picks, beaters, sledge hammers and axe-eye mattocks. Hoe, grubbing and digger handles were offered in square, oval and diamond patterns. I had never heard the names of half of these tools, let alone seen them in use. There were several pages of different spade and fork handles and, naturally, there were axe handles. The brochure was a window into another age, the aeon before the mechanization of agriculture, a time that arguably stretched back from the middle of the twentieth century to the beginning of farming.

'My grandfather also sold hundreds of thousands of tool handles to miners in South Wales every year. The company had its own sawmill then,' John said, returning with mugs of tea. The mines declined, though, while modern, manmade materials gradually replaced ash during the twentieth century. John's father had had to diversify to stay in business. He produced ash for the production of tennis, squash and badminton rackets, lacrosse sticks, croquet mallets, snooker cue rests, slip-catch cradle laths and cricket stumps, as well as 'bends' for hockey sticks.

'It's fantastic stuff, ash. It's just so versatile,' John said as we sipped our tea. I closed the brochure. John tapped a thick finger on the illustration in the middle of the front cover: it depicted a Stone Age man fashioning the haft for a hand axe out of a piece of ash. 'At the end of the Second World War, there were forty-four tool-manufacturing businesses in Great Britain. Now there are two. And really, we're the only exclusive wooden handle-maker left. There's a company in the north of England who still make complete tools, many with wooden handles, and there are a few small businesses and individuals making chisel handles, scythes and the like, but if you want some tool handles from your ash, we're your people,' he continued.

If the 'last of the wooden tool handle-makers' conjures an image from a Thomas Hardy novel of men in smocks and neckerchiefs, working in a cruck-frame barn with swallows flitting in and out, to the calming sound of wood being shaved by hand, then the modern-day reality will be a shock. A. S. Lloyd & Son is based in a small factory on the edge of a light-industrial estate, beside a busy commuter route in the Vale of Glamorgan. The main workshop was heaving with machinery as I carried my pieces of timber in. Circular saws, belt sanders, high-speed polishing machines, dowelling machines and extractor systems were all thrumming, throbbing, whining and whirring in turbulent disagreement.

When we first spoke on the phone, John had told me that his factory had the capacity to manufacture almost 2,000 different wooden products in ash and hickory, including all the subtle variations of the standard articles and the specialist stock for clients like the national rail network and the Ministry of Defence. As the machines have to be reset for each product – a time-consuming part of the process – I would either have to leave my timber at the factory, to be turned into wares of my choice at a later date, or take whatever they were making on the day I turned up. Fortuitously, one of the machines was set up to make 24-inch felling axe handles when I arrived – and this was precisely what I wanted.

John explained that long handles for striking tools like axes, mauls and sledgehammers are often made from hickory these days, which is imported from the USA. Hickory is excellent timber for striking tools: it's a bit tougher than ash, which means you can have a slightly thinner handle. It is, however, a bit heavier to handle and it's harder on the saws. 'With a 36-inch sledgehammer handle, for example, hickory will probably last a bit longer than ash. But when you come down to a 12-, 14- or 16-inch hammer handle, ash is going to last just as long, if you don't misuse it, of course. And for long, lifting tools rather than striking tools – implements that have to take a steady strain like hay forks, manure forks or West of England shovels, anything over 36 inches – ash is without doubt the best. It's the same in America. They use hickory for striking handles and white ash for non-striking tool handles,' John told me, eyeing my timber, which I had stacked on the floor.

We lifted one of the boards onto a metal bench. John looked at it closely. I wondered how many pieces of ash he'd examined during his twenty-five years in the business. As a young man, John nearly became a professional golfer, before turning to engineering. That led to a decade working for rally car teams on the international circuit. Eventually the pull of the family business became too great, but the adventures didn't end when he joined A. S. Lloyd & Son. John had numerous, bizarre stories about setting up wood-turning factories in Lithuania immediately after the Berlin Wall came down, and selling tool handles to the Red Army in Soviet Russia. He seemed to have visited everywhere in Europe where common ash grows well, and he had connections through ash in the Ardennes Forest, Poland, Lithuania, Croatia and Slovenia.

'It's good ash-growing country where you live on the Welsh Borders, Rob, and this timber looks OK,' John said, running an index finger across the grain. 'It's certainly good enough to make 24-inch felling axe handles. Critically, when it's sawn, we have to ensure that the grain runs straight through your handles, from top to bottom. This is very important for strength. One criticism might be that the growth rings in this piece of timber are quite close together. You do know that faster-grown ash, with wider-spaced growth rings, is stronger, don't you?'

The mechanical or 'strength' properties of materials constitute a complex but important field of science. Even understanding a basic material like, say, steel, is complicated, though a piece of well-made steel is both uniform in its composition and its properties are equal in all directions. Wood, on the other hand, is not uniform in composition: it is an organic product of infinite variation in detail. It is subject to differences between species, genetic variability within the same species, variance according to growing conditions and a host of other irregularities. Fundamentally, wood is also 'anisotropic' – its mechanical properties may be very different when measured in different directions, namely longitudinal (parallel to the grain), radial (perpendicular to the grain, through the centre of a round piece of wood) and tangential (perpendicular to the grain but tangential to the growth rings).

The density or the weight for a given volume of wood varies greatly between tree species. This is important because density is a key factor in determining a wood's strength properties. The density of balsa, the lightest of all commercial woods, for example, is 200 kg per cubic metre; lignum vitae, at the other end of the scale, is six times denser at around 1200 kg per cubic metre. Ash sits near the middle, at 690 kg per cubic metre. All these figures are for wood with 12 per cent moisture content – the standard for strength testing and density measurements. However, because of the variability of wood, the figures are merely approximations based on average species characteristics – they are for guidance.

The density of different pieces of wood from the same tree will even vary: wood at the base is familiarly more dense than wood higher up the trunk, while wood midway between the pith, the small core of soft tissue at the centre of a stem or branch, and the bark tends to be denser than either the centre or the outside. In ring-porous, hardwood species like oak, hickory and ash, wood density also varies between the early-wood and the latewood tissue contained within a single, annual growth ring. Examined under a microscope, the cells of the earlywood are seen to have thin walls and large vessels or pores, while latewood is made up of more woody substance and fewer holes. Thus, latewood is denser than earlywood. As faster-grown trees have a higher proportion of latewood to earlywood, it follows they are denser than slower-grown trees of the same species. How fast a tree grows is determined by a number of factors including genetic stock, soil quality, how the trees are planted, climatic conditions and management techniques.

Density affects several mechanical properties of wood, one of which is particularly associated with tool handles. The complex property known to scientists as 'toughness' is the ability of a material to absorb energy under the impact of a sudden blow and undergo deformation without fracturing or cracking. Toughness is basically shock-resistance, and research has shown that it increases proportionally with density in ring-porous hardwoods. Toughness requires a combination of strength and ductility or pliability. Materials like ceramics, for example, are not 'tough': they are strong but brittle, as they have limited ductility or pliability.

Toughness in wood also varies significantly between species. However, several thousand years after man first understood that some timber species resist sudden impact better than others, we still don't entirely understand why. It relates to the molecular structure of the cell walls in a tree, yet authorities in wood science can't agree which part of these structures determines toughness. Whatever the reasons, toughness is an essential requirement in timber for the manufacture of tool handles. It is an outstanding property particularly associated with two species: hickory and ash. They can absorb sudden impact forces that would break almost all other woods.

Because the density of wood is so variable, timber from different ash trees is irregularly resistant to shock. However, the speed at which a tree grows gives you a good indication as to its toughness. And – this is the beautiful bit – you only have to count the number of growth rings per inch on a piece of timber, by placing a ruler perpendicular to the grain, to assess the speed of growth. If the rings are very close together – say, twenty or more per inch – then you know the tree has grown slowly; if the rings are wider apart – less than ten rings per inch – a tree is considered fast grown. 'The highest quality ash, for things like ladder rungs, sporting goods and the best tool handles, must have a growth rate of four to sixteen rings per inch,' John told me. 'Your timber is on the edge of that, but I think you'll be OK making tool handles out of it. Let's give it a go.'

Taking a piece of wood in the shape of a standard, 24-inch axe handle, Richard, one of John's employees, began to mark out shapes in pencil on my timber. He managed to squeeze in the outlines of six axe handles. On the band saw, he manoeuvred the timber across the polished steel table, smoothly guiding the pencil markings into the teeth of the blade. The small offcuts were swept into a bucket: they would keep the wood-burner in the office stoked over winter. I knew the bigger offcuts wouldn't go to waste either. Because of the great variety in the size of the wares made at A. S. Lloyd & Son, from pull switches and dibbers (small hand tools for planting seeds) to long rake handles, the conversion rate from timber to product is very high. John had told me that he even insisted on taking the flitches from the sawmills because he might get a few small items out of them.

After ten minutes, the rough blanks were all cut to shape. Using a home-made centring device and a hammer, Richard whacked pinholes into the ends of each piece of wood and fixed three of them in place on the copying lathe, a machine used to reproduce the plane and curved surfaces of products by mimicking a template. The 'master' axe handle was already on the lathe. The pieces of ash began to turn in unison: as a stylus traced the master, the banks of cutters responded, moving in and out of my ash pieces, slowly reshaping them in the image of the template. Chips flew. After five minutes, three handles emerged. After ten minutes there were six. A piece was nicked off the bottom or 'knob' of each handle on a circular saw, to give it the right shape.

Michael, who has worked at A. S. Lloyd & Son for forty years, gathered the handles and carried them across the workshop to the belt sander. The machine chugged to life, like an old smoker of Gauloises clearing his throat. Michael examined one of the handles. From the way his lips pursed, I could tell my timber passed the inspection, but only just.

He raised the handle and offered it to me. 'Feel a little dampness in there, can't you?' he said.

I couldn't feel a thing. I gripped tightly around the 'throat' of the handle – nothing. I tried further up, around the 'belly' – still nothing. I wasn't even sure what I was supposed to feel. It crossed my mind that he was pulling my leg.

Michael took the handle back. 'I'd say it'll be fine. Just a bit of dampness,' he said.

John had earlier told me that Michael's knowledge and understanding of the timber was profound. He thought that by the time each billet of ash has been sawn, turned, sanded and polished into a final product, Michael would have intuitively run 200 visual checks on it. I delighted in the thought that you could put Michael in Dr Who's Tardis and transport him through time to any period in the last 7,000 years, anywhere in Europe or North America, and his singular intimacy with ash would find him work.

Michael pressed the handle on the revolving belt of sandpaper. The fibres in the ash hissed against the abrasive grit. He rolled the handle over and over in his hands, like a pool player turning a cue before a shot. Sometimes he pressed hard, defining the veins in his forearms, and a breath of dust flew off the handle. At other times, he dabbed the ash delicately on the belt. When every curve was smooth, the strokes got shorter and more infrequent. The first handle was done. Without looking up, he gathered the next handle and began the same choreographed sequence of sweeps and swipes. After fifteen minutes, all the handles were sanded down and ready to be waxed.

*

Putting the axe handles into the boot of my car, I thought of something Jacquetta Hawkes wrote in her majestic book, *A Land*: 'I know of only one traditional form for an everyday tool which has been adapted without loss to machine production; this is the exquisitely curved and modulated handle of the wood-cutter's axe.' I held one of the handles. I ran my hand down from the shoulder, over the belly and across the throat to the knob. It really was 'exquisitely curved', but there was great purpose about it too. The handle felt ready to work. I didn't know if this was the compound residue of the tens of millions of axe handles made from ash over the ages, ending in this millimetre-perfect ergonomic shape – or if it was simply the woodland calling me.

'You'll find it works better with an axe-head on the end,' John said, stepping out of the office door to say goodbye. He had spent the afternoon setting up one of his machines to manufacture a brand-new product – a stonemason's mallet. It would be low volume, he explained, but it was still new business.

'I suppose I shouldn't be surprised. The properties of ash remain the same. It should be as valued today as it was millennia ago,' he said, shaking my hand. 'You'll get many years of good use out of that handle. Now I've said that, you'll probably go and break it next week.'

CHAPTER 3

Keep Cart on Wheel

'The grain of the wood told secrets to them.'
George Sturt, *The Wheelwright's Shop*

'Beautiful stuff that. Beautiful,' Phill Gregson said, admiring the planks of ash as we hauled them out of the back of my van into bright sunshine. 'Straight as a die. The sawmilling on it is good. It'll make lovely felloes. Much appreciated. Granddad,' he called over his shoulder, 'come and have a look at this.'

Phill is a wheelwright, an almost extinct craftsperson with the skills and ability to make the wooden and metal parts of wheels, as well as the wagons, carts and other vehicles the wheels are mounted on. At thirty years old, Phill has been in the family trade for a decade, but he's been familiar with wheelwrighting from birth. His father was a wheelwright. His mother was a wheelwright from the day she left school until Phill was born. Both Phill's grandfather, who was idling his way across the yard towards us, and his great-grandfather were wheelwrights too. In a tradition that is almost unheard of now, the same family have been associated with the same ancient craft from the end of the nineteenth century to the present day.

'It's nice to have that history. The little bits of knowledge

68

and skill that are handed down by word of mouth, they're invaluable,' Phill said, still staring at the timber, searching the grain for the secrets.

Phill and I had first spoken on the telephone. Driving north to visit him in an isolated corner of England, on the Lancashire coast, I had half expected to meet a hulking man with the physique of a Turkish wrestler and a fierce gaze. In fact, he was slight with a pop star's mop of brown hair, goofy teeth and a warm smile. Immediately, I knew him to be as straightforward in character as the grain in the ash planks we were admiring. One thing I had correctly surmised, from reading about the history of wheelwrighting, was that Phill would know his timber.

'The wheelwrights had a sort of connoisseur's interest in the timber,' George Sturt wrote in his much-loved monograph of the craft, *The Wheelwright's Shop*, published in 1930. Sturt would have known his timber too: he was a coach-builder by trade. The wheelwright's knowledge of timber goes beyond the information set out in books. It is a feel for the characteristics of the different tree species, including ash, which was always used for the felloes (it rhymes with 'bellies') or rims of the wheels, gained through lengthy empirical acquaintance. It is knowing about seasoning and where a knot will be helpful, or a bit of shake a source of unexpected strength. This intimate understanding of timber was passed down from father to son, and from master to apprentice, like oral folk-songs. This consciousness of materials forms a continuum in the history of making wheels, connecting Phill to the earliest wheelwrights in ancient Mesopotamia, over 5,000 years ago. I knew if the timber from my ash tree was to be critically examined anywhere, it would be here, in the wheelwright's yard.

'If you're making a wheel that might last a century, or longer, then selecting good timber is essential,' Phill said as we lifted the first plank onto the front of his tractor. I had brought four pieces of ash: two boards 3 inches thick and 6 foot long; one board 2 inches thick by 6 foot and a 1-inch-thick board by 8 foot. All four boards were the width of the tree and still had the bark on. 'This 1-inch board has got lovely, straight grain. I'll steam-bend it, to make some wooden bicycle wheels. The 3-inch will be used for wide felloes, to make the wheels for a heavy haulage wagon,' Phill said, hopping between the boards. 'The 2-inch will make felloes for light-duty wheels, for small-ish gypsy wagons and the like. There are a couple of knots here but we can make best use of them by cutting a felloe out using the contour of the grain around the knot. A 6-foot board – I'll get twenty odd felloes out of that, maybe more. I don't often come across British ash as good as this. What d'you think, Granddad?'

Edward Crowhurst had arrived next to us. He was wearing work boots, brown corduroy trousers, a green sweatshirt rolled up to the elbows, a white cloth apron and a battered, black and white houndstooth trilby hat. A wooden ruler with a metal hinge poked out of his rear trouser pocket. I asked if he was still wheelwrighting.

'No, no,' Edward said. 'I gave that game up. I'm eighty-six years old. I'm still working, though. I'm making a chair now, for Phillip. I like doing it. I'm one of the lucky people, me. All my life I've done what I like doing. Making something with your hands gives you peace of mind. And the pleasure you get when someone comes in and says, "By gum, you've made a good job of that." Now, let's see this timber.' He placed a hand on the sapwood, gleaming white in the morning sun, and ran his hand up and down the grain. It was an instinctive act of affection for the smooth, warm wood. 'Don't see ash like this very often, at least not round here,' Edward said. 'They grow lettuce round here, not trees.'

Phill and Edward's yard was a fenced camp beside a single-track lane, a few miles from the village of Mere Brow, near Southport on the Irish Sea coast. There was a barn with a couple of workshops and a flat where Phill lived, a small sawmill and various other sheds, lean-tos and outhouses. There was no signage outside the yard on the lane: like crafts-people through the ages, Phill clearly relied on his reputation to bring him all the work he needed.

The surrounding area was the largest lake in England at the end of the Middle Ages, called Martin Mere. In the nineteenth century, the drainage of the marshlands left a swathe of fine agricultural land. Farming vegetables and flowers, rather than forestry, remains the most important local industry today.

'This is what it doesn't like, the sun,' Edward said, swiping the palm of his hand across the face of the timber again and brushing a film of fine dust off: 'Wood doesn't like sun. How long has the timber been seasoning for, young man?'

There are several reasons for 'seasoning' or drying timber. Seasoned wood is lighter: a green piece of beech, for example, weighs twice as much as the same piece when it is completely dry, while ash loses almost a third of its weight. Lighter wood is, of course, easier to handle and transport. Also, dry wood is significantly more resistant to decay and it generally takes preservatives, paints and polishes better. For wheelwrights, as well as a multitude of other woodworkers of diverse crafts and trades, there are more important reasons for seasoning timber, though: wood is both stronger and more stable when it has been correctly dried. 'Seasoning' is, then, a fundamental part of the process of converting a tree into artefacts and products. It is as important as felling the tree correctly. Knowledge, care and a little artistry are required to get it right.

'A year for every inch of thickness plus a year for the tree – that's a reasonable guide. It's a long old process, seasoning. If you bring me a 3-inch board of ash, I won't use it for at least four years,' Phill had said when I telephoned. I wasn't surprised. I had read about wheelwrights who seasoned pieces of timber for ten years before using them.

Wood is a hygroscopic material: it is constantly trying to attain a state of equilibrium with the air surrounding it. A growing tree contains large quantities of water. The amount of water varies greatly between species. No matter what the species, though, the moisture begins to evaporate when the tree is felled and planked, and air comes into contact with the wood. If air can circulate freely, the timber will continue to lose moisture by evaporation: as the water is pulled out of the exterior layers of a piece of wood, the deeper water gets pulled towards the surface so the whole thickness dries, until equilibrium between moisture in the surface layers of the timber and moisture in the air surrounding it is established.

As moisture is removed, the strength of the wood remains approximately constant until all the moisture that actually fills the cells is gone; thereafter, as a small part of the moisture present in the structural cell walls of the wood is drawn out, strength increases progressively, and in some species considerably.

Equally important for the wheelwright is the fact that removing moisture causes the timber to shrink. The shrinkage continues until the timber has reached equilibrium with the surrounding atmosphere. At this point, the timber is deemed to be stable, and it may be put to use.

Today, it is common practice for sawmills to dry timber in kilns, which speeds the process up considerably. The cheapest and simplest way to season timber, however, is to air dry it. The best time to stack hardwood timber for drying is early winter: cool temperatures and, more importantly, relatively high humidity ensures the drying process is gentle over the first few months, when the risk of seasoning timber too quickly is greatest. If timber is seasoned too fast, it is more likely to twist, warp and split, which constrains how it may be used and reduces the value.

After my tree was felled, I had waited several weeks for the haulier to show up. There were then further, unexpected delays at the sawmill and it was the end of spring when the trunk was finally sawn into boards. 'Stacking your timber to dry at this time of year is far from ideal, but you might just get away with it,' Will Bullough at Whitney Sawmills had said. 'Keep your fingers crossed we have a cold, damp start to the summer.'

Two days later, a heatwave began. On instructions from Will, I stacked my tree (or 'put it in stick' as he said) in the barn beside my house, in 'log form' – effectively the same shape as it was before being sawn into planks. The planks were separated with 1-inch by 1-inch sticks, placed a foot apart along each board – to 'let the weather in', as the old expression goes, and to restrict some of the warping liable to occur as a result of the shrinkage. The large doors on both sides of the barn were wedged open to allow air to circulate freely. I hung drapes over the doors, to prevent sunlight falling directly onto the timber. I sat by, nervously waiting. While the rest of the country basked in the finest spell of hot weather for a decade, I silently prayed for rain.

Seasoning timber is further complicated by the fact that natural shrinkage during the drying process does not occur in equal amounts in every direction. Shrinkage along the length of the tree is insignificant and commonly disregarded. Looking at a cross section of a tree, the greatest shrinkage happens tangentially to the direction of the annual growth rings. Radial shrinkage, in a direction from the centre of the tree outwards, is nearly always less than tangential shrinkage. A plank that comes from near the centre of a log will undergo different degrees of shrinkage on its two sides: the top side, furthest from the heart of the tree, experiences nearly full tangential shrinkage, while the bottom side undergoes a mix of radial and tangential shrinkage. As it dries, the plank will want to become concave on the topside, and it will warp or 'cup'.

By the end of summer, one of my boards had cupped

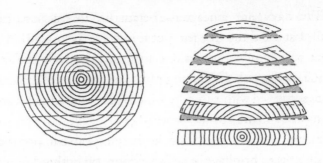

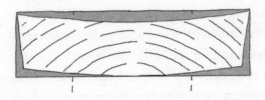

Cupping of a flat sawn board

noticeably. Some planks sawn from the centre of the tree had split at the ends. This was, Will had told me, likely to happen. Otherwise, my boards of ash were all intact, straight, flat or very nearly flat and drying out evenly – a matter of huge relief. The timber from the split and cupped boards could still be used, of course: I would just have to be a bit more creative about finding that wood a home.

That I had got away with it was partly to do with the sound advice Will had given me, and partly to do with the properties of ash. Species like sycamore and elm should, initially at least, be seasoned at low temperatures and relatively high humidity, or the timber will darken and warp. Oak has higher moisture content and a denser structure than ash: it splits easily if dried too fast when green. Ash, on the other hand, is more tolerant of a little carelessness during the drying process. Like a good marriage, there is plenty of give before a rupture takes place.

'Come in, come in,' Phill said, leading me into his workshop. 'I never quite got the place sorted after moving in ... and I moved in ten years ago.'

Blocks and planks of timber were stacked under several wooden workstations and along two walls. Mounds of sawdust and wood chips rested around the saw benches. Pieces of Victorian machinery lay on the floor. There were drawers of hand-turning tools, hoops of iron, vices, lathes, planers, jigs, gauges, routers, saw horses, strips of steel, a trammel, spokes, hammers, rulers, mandrels, boxes with steel bits spilling out and old wheels. A rusting trials motorbike was slowly being fenced into a corner by piles of anonymous clutter.

'As long as you know where everything is,' I said, slowly taking in the chaos.

'I wish I did,' Phill replied.

In the end room, watery sunshine poured through a large window onto the workbench. Phill stopped and turned, with his fists resting on his hips, silhouetted by the light: 'Shall we make a wheel then?'

He had explained on the phone that it takes the best part of three days to make a single wooden wheel – longer than he wanted me hanging around his workshop, asking questions

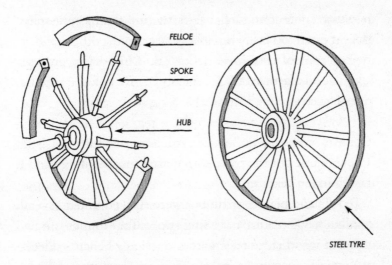

FELLOE

SPOKE

HUB

STEEL TYRE

and getting in the way. He was in the middle of making a set of four twelve-spoke cartwheels: as I was particularly interested in the ash felloes, he kindly agreed to prepare the hub and the spokes of a wheel before I arrived.

Several hubs, also called 'naves' or 'stocks', were lined up on the bench in the sunlight. The wheel currently being made was clamped horizontally, face-down on a 'wheel stool'. Traditionally, Phill explained, naves were made of English elm in Britain, because of its high tensile strength in all directions, and resistance to splitting. When Dutch elm disease all but eradicated the species in the 1970s, wheelwrights were forced to find an alternative.

'I'm like a magpie for elm trees,' Phill said. 'I'd love to be able to use elm but the elms that grow now don't quite get big enough for naves. Sad, isn't it? I will use elm if the job has to be historically accurate but I tend to use utile, an African hardwood, in its place. It has a similar interlocking grain structure to elm and is very durable.'

The spokes were made from oak. Phill still shapes his spokes entirely by hand, for maximum strength. The holes, called 'mortices', had already been cut in the nave; the shoulders of the twelve spokes, called 'tenons', had also been prepared. These joints between the nave and the spokes, Phill explained, are of paramount importance to the strength and true running of the wheel. He carefully measured each mortice with a divider before taking final shavings off the tenons with a hand plane. He took the first spoke, spat on a tenon and drove it into the mortice with a one-handed, short-handle sledgehammer, checking the joint carefully after each blow.

'The spit stops the spoke bouncing back and helps the wood grip. Same reason you spit on your hands before picking up a hammer,' Phill said.

When the last spoke had been thwacked into the nave, the 'spider' (or 'speech', a delightful and now forgotten word from the arcane language of wheelwrighting) was complete. The wheel was starting to take shape.

The spokes were then cut to the correct length on a band saw. Phill showed me the machine that would cut the tenons, or 'tangs' as he called them, onto the spoke ends. These would eventually fit into the felloes.

'It's basically a hollow auger or borer that cuts round tenons on the spoke ends. A friend of Granddad's built it out of a washing machine, a bit of a petrol pump, a drill and the wheel of an old Morris Minor. We're full of barmy ideas here. We tend to dream the machines up and then go and make them.'

When all the tangs were cut, the workshop was quiet again. The flecks of oak settled in piles on the floor. Phill stretched his back. He was ready to cut the ash felloes.

The wooden wheel is one of the greatest technological advances in the chronicle of the human race: its history is the history of civilization. The consensus is that the wheel was invented around 5,500 years ago, between the Tigris and Euphrates Rivers in Mesopotamia, part of modern Iraq. The earliest indication of the use of wheeled vehicles is a sketch of a sledge mounted on four wheels, in a Sumerian tablet found in this region, the 'Fertile Crescent' of the ancient world, and dated to around 3,500 BC. The first wheels were solid. They were cross sections cut from the trunk of a tree; because the natural strength of the grain, which runs from end to end of a trunk, was not utilized, solid wheels were inherently flawed.

The next, great evolutionary step came around 1,700 BC, when Egyptian carpenters developed the composite wooden wheel made of felloes carved from individual wooden pieces, radial spokes and hubs, all connected by mortice and tenon joints. These wheels were mounted on horse-drawn chariots. Light and easily manoeuvred, the chariots revolutionized military tactics and were the decisive factor in great wars between empires. Several chariots, such as the one discovered in the tomb of the boy-pharaoh Tutankhamun, who ruled Egypt circa 1332–1323 BC, survive complete. They are masterpieces of early wheelwrighting ingenuity. Interestingly, the cabs of these chariots commonly comprised frames of steam-bent elm or ash; the axles were usually made from ash, as were the felloes. Ash doesn't grow in Egypt, but we know from records that it was imported from Europe.

During the Iron Age, the spoked wooden wheel reached a highly developed state throughout Europe, giving land transport a characteristic and predictable pace that lasted until the Industrial Revolution. Wheelwrights with extensive knowledge of timber used different species for different components of the wheel. Spokes became narrower; felloes were trimmed, to reduce weight; the whole wheel was often 'hooped' with a shrink-fitted, circular band of iron, to brace the wheel together and provide a protective sheath.

The Roman wooden chariot wheel discovered during an archaeological dig at Bar Hill Fort in Scotland, and dated to around AD 150, is a well-preserved example of an Iron Age wheel. The hub is made from elm, and the felloe is made from a single piece of ash, bent into a circle through the process of artificially softening the wood using steam. Similar wheels have been discovered along Hadrian's Wall and at La Tène, near Lake Neuchâtel in the Swiss Alps, while an excellent example of an Iron Age wheel – comprising a birch hub, oak spokes and six, sectional ash felloes – was discovered at Holme Pierrepont in Nottinghamshire.

Until the invention of the metal, tension-spoked wheel in the late nineteenth century, the vast majority of wheels were made from wood, using the methods perfected by Iron Age wheelwrights. Almost all carts, chariots, carriages, coaches, drays, barrows, barouches, traps, tumbrils, rickshaws, gigs, haywains, buggies, curricles, chaises, broughams, troikas and wagons had wheels constructed with ash rims. Many of these diverse vehicles would have had axles and shafts made from ash too.

At the end of the Middle Ages, the wagons themselves were even made from ash. While oak was traditionally used in vehicles pulled by oxen, ash was preferred for the framework of horse-drawn coaches, because it was lighter to pull and more comfortable to travel on. The writer, poet and River Thames waterman John Taylor wrote in his diatribe against coachmen, *The World Runnes on Wheels*, published in 1623: 'The [coaches] have beene the universall decay of almost all the best Ash Trees in the kingdome, for a young plant can no sooner peepe up to any perfection, but presently it is felled for a Coach.'

The distinct craft of coach-building with ash originated in the sixteenth century, but it snowballed in Britain with the expansion of the road system at the end of the eighteenth century. Increasing prosperity and the growth of the middle class meant coach-building flourished again during the second half of the nineteenth century. In 1874, there were 432,000 carriages in use in Britain. During the 1880s, 40,000 horse-drawn vehicles were handmade each year: almost every one had an ash frame. The Coachbuilders' Association frequently appealed to the Board of Agriculture, to encourage landowners to grow more ash and grow it better. The same story is repeated across Europe.

The role of ash in transportation did not end with the demise of the 'horse age', though. When Karl Benz invented the motor car in 1885, coach-builders quickly realized they could adapt their trade to this new conveyance. For the next thirty years, most car bodies were built around an ash frame. At least, wherever good ash grew, they were: coach-building companies on the Continent without access to supplies of domestically grown ash tended to use European beech instead – an inferior alternative.

When Dodge introduced the first mass-produced car with an all-steel body in 1917, the tradition of manufacturing motor-body frames from ash in the USA declined steeply. In Europe, car manufacturers were slower to adopt new materials and technology: oak bottom sides, ash frames, aluminium panels and steel wings remained the norm in the years after the First World War. The number of British coach-builders only really began to dwindle in the 1930s, when the larger car manufacturers emerged with the means of mass production and in-house, pressed-steel-body workshops. Hand-built, bespoke wooden car bodies were still produced, but the role of ash in the construction of elite motor cars was waning too. Jaguar launched their first all-steel-body car in 1938: at the time, the company still owned a sawmill, to process the large quantities of ash timber they required. Rolls-Royce switched to pressed-steel bodywork in 1944.

While the wartime aviation industry created the famous de Havilland Mosquito, a combat aircraft constructed partly from ash and known as the 'Wooden Wonder', it also developed the expertise to machine low-volume body parts and extrude light alloys, which was the death knell for ash car bodies. In *Trees, Woods and Man*, published in 1956, H. L. Edlin noted: 'In motor-body building, especially in the framing of buses and vans, ash is highly prized, because it bends well and gives great strength and shock absorption.' In truth, this was the wooden coach-builders' last gasp.

London's iconic Routemaster buses were still built with ash structural bodies in the 1960s, as were a great number of railway wagons. Ash was used for the bodywork on the much-loved Morris 1000 Travellers into the 1970s, but the numbers were only small. By 1970, the role of timber in the motor industry was effectively redundant. With that, the millennia-old association between ash and human transportation quietly ended.

Well, almost ended. The Morgan Motor Company, a boutique British sports car manufacturer founded in 1910, still uses ash in the bespoke production of sports cars. In a process the company calls 'twenty-first-century coach-building', the passenger compartments of cars are constructed with an ash frame and alloy outer body panels, on an aluminium or steel chassis. This tradition-based method of motor car body-building became an anachronism towards the end of the twentieth century. Today, however, such craftsmanship is increasingly valued again and the Morgan Motor Company is thriving.

For centuries, wheelwright shops were as common as garages are today: 'I can remember when there was one on every corner,' Edward, Phill's grandfather, had told me. In 1911, at the apex of the horse age, there were, according to the England and Wales census, 23,785 wheelwrights and 1,200 apprentices. The craft of wheelwrighting declined during the twentieth century, in parallel with the number of farm and commercial horses in use. At the peak before the First

World War, there were over two million working horses in England and Wales; by 1965, the number of agricultural horses was down to 20,000. The wheelwright, once an essential craftsperson in every village and community, all but vanished. A survey in 1980 put the number of working wheelwrights in the UK at twenty-five.

Phill is a Master Wheelwright and a Yeoman of the Worshipful Company of Wheelwrights in London. The Company supports what is left of the trade and keeps the history, while there is a plan to set up an apprentice scheme. Phill always has a year's worth of orders in the book. He makes wheels for gypsy wagons, brewery drays, shrimping carts, heavy haulage vehicles, steam wagons and haywains. He works for private customers, museums and occasionally film production companies, but he is busy partly because there are so few wheelwrights left.

'It's no longer a living tradition. There's not even a wheelwright in every county and I believe I'm the youngest by some way. There's very little written down in books and anyway, there's so much about the job that you wouldn't even think to write down. It'll all be gone very, very quickly. There's an old saying – "Wheelwrights never retire, they just die" – but I do worry that the skill of hundreds of generations of wheelwrights won't be passed on. The use of ash for the felloes in wooden wheels has been a constant for at least 2,500 years, wherever ash grows. All that knowledge of the timber . . . gone. I'll keep at it, but it's a bit depressing when you think about it,' Phill said.

*

As I was getting my camera from the van, Phill appeared in the doorway of the workshop, rolling an old, twelve-spoke cartwheel weighing 30 kilos, which he'd recently repaired. When he had my attention, he gripped the top of the wheel, hoisted it 50 centimetres off the ground and let go. It smacked on the stone floor and – to my astonishment – bounced 20 centimetres back into the air.

The fact that the wheel bounced said much about the skill of the wheelwright who originally made it. It also reminded me about one of the most important physical properties of ash – elasticity. When engineers talk about elasticity in wood, they are generally referring to its ability – when deformed or forced out of shape – to regain its original shape, as a wheel felloe does when it rolls over a stone in the road. The opposite of elasticity is brittleness. Hickory and ash are notably elastic species, while poplar and American white pine, for example, are well known for being brittle.

In materials science, elasticity is measured by something called the 'modulus of elasticity', also known as 'Young's Modulus' (after the nineteenth-century British scientist Thomas Young), and generally abbreviated to 'E' or 'MOE'. The MOE is a good overall indicator of the strength of a piece of wood and it is a measurement commonly used in the timber industry, particularly with respect to structural timber. It is worth understanding how it is calculated.

If you apply a small load to a piece of wood, the strain put on the wood will cause it to deform slightly, internally; it will then return to its original shape when the load is removed. If you add further small loads, the increased strain will cause the wood to deform further in small increments that are proportional to the load, and then again to recover when the load is removed. In other words, the amount of load applied divided by the amount of deformation is a constant. At least, it is a constant up to a tipping point called the 'limit of proportionality'. A piece of wood can be said to be 'elastic' up to this limit. Beyond the limit, the sample of wood will not return to its original shape when the load is removed: it will be permanently deformed, since some of the cell walls in the wood have been crushed or ruptured.

The value of this constant below the limit of proportionality will naturally vary according to the size of the sample of wood. It is necessary, therefore, to express the load in terms of the cross-sectional area it is applied to, and deformation in terms of the initial length of the piece of wood. So the load (measured in a unit of force called a Newton or N) divided by the cross-sectional area of wood (mm^2) gives you a figure for what scientists call 'stress' (N/mm^2); deformation (mm) divided by the original length (mm) gives you a figure for 'strain'. Stress divided by strain gives us the 'modulus of elasticity'. It is measured in N/mm^2.

Because wood has independent mechanical properties in three different directions, the MOE of a piece can be calculated in three ways. However, the longitudinal (parallel to the grain) MOE is the most important. It has been most exhaustively tested for in materials science and is the figure commonly given as the guideline MOE for a piece of wood in the timber industry. The MOE characterizes that one piece of wood. The MOE will be similar for other pieces of wood from the same part of the same tree, but it varies through an entire tree and within a species, because wood is a natural material and subject to many influences. MOE also varies significantly between different tree species. In practical terms, the MOE number itself isn't that meaningful, but it is useful in comparison with other woods because it tells us something about the relative properties of the different species.

The higher the MOE value then, the more elastic the wood is. Common ash has a relatively high MOE value, higher than elm, plane, sycamore, sweet chestnut, alder and oak, for example. Of the common European hardwoods, only beech and birch have marginally higher values than ash. Why ash has a high MOE can be explained at a cellular level.

With the advent of high-powered, electron microscopes in the middle of the twentieth century, scientists were able to study the size, shape, construction and arrangement of the cells in wood for the first time; this led to great advances in our understanding of how the cellular structure in wood relates to its mechanical properties. We now know that the walls of the cells in wood are made up of a primary wall and a secondary wall, which is composed of three layers. The middle layer of the secondary wall, prosaically called 'S2', is the thickest and most important part of the cell: it has the greatest effect on how that cell behaves and on the physical properties of that piece of wood.

The S2 layer is largely comprised of cellulose, which is laid down in chains of tiny fibres called 'microfibrils'. These fibres wind around the cells, spiralling upwards, a bit like the coils of a spring. The angle at which the microfibrils spiral in relation to the main axis of the cell, which is parallel to the direction the tree grows, is called the microfibril angle or 'MFA', and it is very important. The MFA of the S2 layer is recognized as one of the main determinants of the mechanical properties of wood, including the modulus of elasticity. Generally speaking, the lower the MFA, the more elastic the timber will be; the higher the MFA, the stiffer the timber will be. Ash has a low MFA. The MFA itself is a biological function of the tree species and, like the modulus of elasticity, it varies a small amount within a single tree and significantly between species.

Although wood has been used exhaustively as an engineering material for millennia, we have only recently begun to appreciate just how extraordinarily complex its cellular structure is. Research into the relationship between microfibril angles and the properties of different wood species is only twenty years or so old, and we still have a great deal to learn.

When Phill had regained control of the wheel, he hoisted and dropped it again. With another great smack, it rebounded

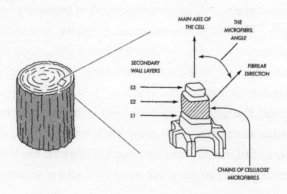

off the floor into his hands: 'Look at that natural spring. That's why we use ash for the felloes. Amazing to think they worked it out thousands of years ago,' he said.

Back inside the workshop, Phill marked the curved outlines of six felloes on a 2-inch-thick, seasoned ash plank. Each felloe was roughly cut on a band saw, planed on one side and passed through a machine called a 'thicknesser', which shaved off any cupping that occurred while the timber was drying and ensured the sides were parallel.

'In this country, it's traditional to build a wheel with one felloe for every two spokes. In other countries, the USA for example, they'll often use a single, steam-bent felloe for the whole wheel, but they're harder to repair. One function of a wooden wheel is that it has to be repairable. It's no good if you just get a tiny bit of rot in a spoke and you then have to replace the whole rim, is it?' Phill said.

The ash felloes were carefully cut to the shape of the pencil markings on the band saw. With each cut a small wedge of ash dropped onto the floor at Phill's feet. 'There's quite a lot of offcuts when you're cutting out felloes, but it all gets used,' he said. 'There's no such thing as waste, just expensive firewood.'

The inner face or 'belly' of the felloes were planed using a disc sander, to remove the saw marks. In the old days, Phill explained, the felloes would have been shaped with axes and adzes. He was taught to do everything by hand first; so if the machines fail, he can still use the hand tools. Phill worked deliberately and precisely. He measured and re-measured; he made markings in pencil, then he checked them, thickening the graphite dash he had already made, then he checked his measurements again. In every movement and act there was evidence of craftsmanship – the basic and enduring impulse to do a job well, for its own sake.

The 'speech' was placed face down on the wheel stool and the first felloe was marked with a bevel, for a cut to be made midway between two spokes. The next felloe was similarly marked and cut. Soon all the felloes were resting on the spokes. Phill explained that the felloes are cut with small gaps between them called 'joints': when the iron tyre is fitted, the last part of the wheel-building process, the felloes are drawn together to press down on the spokes. If the felloes tighten without maintaining the right degree of pressure on the spokes, the wheel is said to be 'felloe-bound' and it will be weaker. The felloes, marked and numbered, were ready to be bored with holes.

'This is imported American white ash. Two World Wars, poor planting schemes, undermanagement – it's hard to get hold of good ash timber in the UK, and on top of everything else, we've now got ash dieback. It's very hard to get ash like the stuff you brought, Rob. This American ash is pretty good. It's clean; it's straight-grained. It can be like iron sometimes and I think they dry it a bit too quickly, but I'm fussy. When I became a Yeoman of the Company of Wheelwrights, I had to swear an oath – to only use wood of sound condition,' Phill said.

The more I understood about the process, the less Phill spoke. The afternoon passed in a gentle sea of timeless, elemental sounds: the rhythmical rasp of the hand planer as the wood yielded to Phill's wishes; the ringing crack of the mallet; the scrape of Phill's pencil on wood; the plunk of ash touching oak; the caw of the spokeshave on the felloes; and the hiss of sandpaper turning dry ash to dust. The process was exhaustive and protracted: I thought of another line from *The Wheelwright's Shop* – 'Hurry being not so great then as now.' Phill didn't hurry. He was making a wheel for a customer and showing me the process at the same time, but he was engaged in the work for itself. The satisfaction of the wheel coming out right was the reward.

Using a tool called a spoke-dog – a 3-foot-long bar of ash with an iron hook on the end – Phill pressed each pair of spokes together and tapped the felloes on with a hammer. Wooden wedges, with a bit of Phill's spit, were driven into the exposed end of the spoke tangs, to keep the wheel bound until it was hooped. The last felloe was measured, cut, drilled and fitted. Metal slips were tacked in across the felloe-joints, to keep the wheel in line. The outside or 'sole' of the felloes were bevelled, ready for hooping. Using an instrument called a 'traveller', Phill measured the outer circumference of the wheel. He scratched a figure in pencil on the white ash, straightened his back, clasped the wheel in both hands and said: 'We're done.'

The wheel would be 'hooped' with an iron tyre heated in a great fire, in front of a big crowd at a country fair the following weekend. I had witnessed the part of the process I wanted to see, but I was sorry to miss the finale.

'It's the romantic part and very satisfying, at least when it all goes right. Lots of steam and noise as the iron hoop cools in water, shrinks and then binds on the ash. And then, when most folk have gone home, we rake the fire in and sit round having a few beers under the stars. You always meet someone interesting.'

We had wandered out of the workshop into the yard where golden sunlight was illuminating the row of wooden wheels awaiting repair.

'It still surprises me, but I get wheels in which are 150 years old and they're often in almost perfect condition,' Phill said. 'It's only an accident or a bit of woodworm which has brought them to me. And they've been used regularly. In fact, if they are used regularly, they tend to be in better condition.'

I thought of the ash planks that I'd given Phill. In a few years, he'd get sixty or so felloes out of the timber. I wondered if the wheels he would make with my ash might be resting against a wheelwright's shop, awaiting some minor repair, in 2170. Conceivably the life of the timber in use could be longer than the life of the ash tree. To give part of my tree such a distant end was an appealing thought.

CHAPTER 4

Against the Grain

'The wood is sweet – I love it well.'
John Clare, 'Recollections after a Ramble'

A few weeks after my tree was felled, I returned to Callow Hill Wood. For an hour, I clambered over the piles of branch wood around the stump of my tree. I was looking for something in particular – a 3-foot section of ash, 10 to 12 inches in diameter. It had to be straight and without any obvious side branches or other defects. Each time I found a bough close to this specification, I hauled it into a new pile. It was severely cold. When my hands began to slow and my lips cracked, I chose a log, sawed it to length and humped it out of the wood on my shoulder. In the barn at home, I sealed both ends of the log with candle wax, to slow the evaporation of moisture.

This log was destined for Robin Wood, Britain's best-known wood-turner and a luminary of the Heritage Crafts Association. He had agreed to turn a bowl from my ash. When we'd first spoken on the phone, I'd glibly said I would deliver the log to his workshop by train and bicycle. I got some strange looks standing on the platform at Abergavenny station, waiting for the 7.27 a.m. train to Manchester Piccadilly, with my bicycle and a 3-foot-long round of ash sticking out of the top of my old mountaineering rucksack. Waiting for the trans-Pennine train in Manchester, with the log occupying the seat beside me, a man walked past and said: 'I work in the timber distribution business, but I think you're taking things too far.' On the trans-Pennine train, the jovial conductor asked: 'Have you got a ticket for your log?'

I was relieved to see Robin waiting at Edale station, though even he burst into laughter as I walked down the slipway. Wiry, fit-looking, with a tuft of brown hair, square glasses, a gold earring and eager, searching eyes, he had the bearing of a jester.

Robin's workshop is in a stone cowshed or 'byre' at Lee Farm, near Edale in the Derbyshire Peak District. A track leads past the byre, through a gate, straight out onto the peat bogs and heather-clad slopes of Kinder Scout, a hallowed mount of British hill-walkers. A cold wind blew off the hill in gusts, carrying the mournful 'coor-wee, coor-wee' of a curlew from the moors. The wind snapped at my coat as we carried the log to the woodpile. Robin yanked at his chainsaw several times before it came to life, sputtering angrily. He cut a 10-inch section off the log and began examining the exposed end.

For much of human history, most ash would have been cultivated, felled and used before it reached 10 inches in diameter, Robin told me. Only in the modern era of powered saws and heavy haulage equipment have we begun to fell older ash trees and plank them. In medieval times, an ash tree would have been mature at between ten and thirty years. Up to this sort of age, ash grows fast.

'It's a journey of discovery every time you cut a log open,' Robin said, running his index finger across the annual rings towards the patch of darker, stained wood and the pith. 'The grain is very tight on this side, and the pith is off-centre – very typical with branch wood. There's a little split here and a bigger split there, caused by the tree shrinking as it dries. The most obvious way to do a bowl with this piece is to cut the log in two, following the bigger split. Because of where the pith is, it won't be a symmetrical bowl, but that doesn't matter. It'll be interesting.'

Robin prefers to use trunk wood rather than branch wood. Ordinarily, he buys whole trees, then converts and dries the timber himself. He explained that wood has a 'sweet spot' for turning, which means it will cut most cleanly at some point between being unseasoned or 'green' and being dry. His expertise in the different states and stages of drying timber would tell him when.

Robin split the log he had cut with an axe. With metal callipers, he marked the largest circle possible on the exposed, creamy timber. Then he picked up a hand axe and began to slice off the bark.

'You learn to recognize the physical properties of timber by sight and sound and feel,' he said, as the bark began to pile up at his feet. 'With this ash, I got the first feel of it when the chainsaw went in. Now, I'm picking up information using the axe on it. Because the tree grew quite slowly, it's not got the fibrousness you tend to associate with ash. The texture of this wood is more difficult to describe. The fibres cut cleanly, rather than tear. If you took a piece of young ash with, say, four to six growth rings per inch, and sliced a slither off with a knife, you could tie it round your finger – that's how springy, flexible and fibrous it can be. Native Americans used to weave baskets out of white ash splints. Older, slower-grown ash like this would crack or snap.'

With the chainsaw, Robin nicked off the edges of the log, fashioning it into a rough hemisphere. When the saw was silent again, and the latest gust of wind had bowled past us down the valley, he suddenly looked across the stream with intense delight: 'Hear that? "Tchik-tchik." Great-spotted woodpecker. Look, look, there he is.' It was as if he'd never seen a bird before. He gazed at it with boyish enthusiasm before abruptly turning back to the piece of wood balanced on the palm of his hand: 'Where were we?' he said. 'Ah, yes. I think this ash will turn nicely. Let's make a bowl.'

The Iron Age site of Glastonbury Lake Village, which dates from around 2,000 years ago, was excavated in the early 1900s. The wealth of archaeological treasure extracted from the peaty Somerset wetlands included daggers, spearheads, saws, a dug-out canoe, wheel spokes, several wheel hubs and fragments from a collection of turned wooden bowls. One particular fragment belonged to a flat-bottomed bowl carved from a single piece of ash with holes on two sides, which may have supported a handle. The bowl is decorated with incised wooden spirals and whorls with intersecting parallel lines. It must have been a beautiful object – and says much about the Celtic wood-turner's intimacy with the material.

We don't know exactly when wood-turning began, but it

was not widespread in Europe until around 600 BC. Prior to that, wood was commonly used as a material to eat off, but vessels were carved with adzes and flint scrapers and then, during the Bronze Age, with knives. By the time the carpenter at the site of Glastonbury Lake Village was turning ash into a bowl, most domestic utensils, including spoons, plates for serving food, spatulas and loom frames, were made from wood.

The Romans introduced pottery to many parts of Europe, including Britain, but as soon as the Empire collapsed, the culture of woodware was resurrected – and thrived. In fact, for at least a thousand years from AD 500, every man and woman in Europe, from kings and queens to paupers and serfs, ate and drank each day from a wooden vessel turned on a lathe. For the vast majority of people during this period, a wooden bowl was a domestic essential and one of a small number of possessions they owned. These bowls must have been intensely personal, in a way that we can hardly appreciate today. The smell, the feel, the detail in the grain, the knots, the weight, the shape, the size and even the cut of the turner's tools must have been unique and familiar only to the owner.

During this period, turners would have bought trees that were roughly the right size for the artefacts they wanted to make: for a 6-inch-diameter bowl, the ideal tree was 7 inches in diameter. Well-managed coppice woodland produced crops of poles that were good for turning every fifteen to twenty-five years, depending on the soil, species and climate. The turner would have taken the trunk as far up as the first, major side branch: everything above that was fuel. The trunks were cross-cut into logs equal in length to the diameter – just as Robin had cut my ash – and split in half, each log making two hemispherical pieces of wood called 'bowl blanks'. We know the majority of bowls were made in this way from at least the fifth century onwards, from analysis of the growth rings of the bowls that have survived.

Turners inevitably had their favourite species, often determined by what grew well where they lived and worked. Box was regarded as the finest of all bowl-turning timbers: the wood is dense and it cuts very cleanly, but box trees prefer brick soils on dry hills and take 200 years to reach the right size to make a 5-inch bowl. Oak turns well, but it was sought after by a multitude of other woodworkers. Many fruitwoods turn beautifully but they were never in plentiful supply. Birch and aspen turn perfectly well.

The most important species of timber in the turning industry during the Middle Ages were alder, field maple, beech and ash. Light enough to spin on the lathe, these species grew in clean poles in well-managed coppice woodland and they cut cleanly across the end grain. Between AD 500 and 1000, alder was the most popular choice. The timber is white when cut, but it quickly oxidizes, turning a rich, exotic orange, which slowly mellows over the years. The majority of these bowls were simple and functional. Bowls belonging to the nobility, however, were often turned from the woody growths or 'burrs' that form on the outside of maple trees, and they were decorated with steps and silver gilt rim mounts.

After the Norman Conquest of Britain, wooden bowls remained the norm for eating, as the staple food was a vegetable soup called 'pottage'. However, the practice of drinking from wooden cups became common too. Many contemporary accounts refer to *ciphis fraxini* or 'ashen cups' – simple wooden cups made from ash for daily imbibing. Significant archaeological finds of woodware suggest that ash became the most popular bowl-turning timber at the end of the eleventh century and remained so for 300 years. It is difficult to understand why the change took place. A belief may have arisen that alder tainted food and drink more than ash. Ash does not taint food and drink while oak, elm and pine, for example, do, at least initially: Robin told me that no British native hardwood leaves any taint after it has been used and washed several times. More likely, the change was purely cultural: the French knights brought the custom of using ash bowls with them from the Continent and when they settled throughout Britain and Ireland, they were emulated.

The survival of contemporary documents, including household accounts, along with the bowls themselves, yields a good picture of the industry during the medieval period. It was clearly the pinnacle of wood-turning in Europe. A staggering number of bowls were produced – 12,000 were ordered for the Coronation of Richard I alone in 1189. The wealth and status of turners steadily grew: an association or 'craft guild', with regulations governing the practice of turning, was established in 1479. By then, though, the fashion for ash was waning: around the beginning of the sixteenth century, beech replaced ash as the wood of choice for bowls.

By the time the *Mary Rose* (the ninety-one-gun flagship of Henry VIII's Navy) heeled and sank in the Solent in 1545, the officer class on board were eating off pewter plates and dishes. Gentrified folk no longer wished to eat off wood. The demise of wooden tableware, for several centuries the most commonplace and quotidian of all the multifarious ways Europeans used wood, had begun. By the beginning of the eighteenth century, when glazed pottery plates had become affordable to the majority, the wooden bowl as a ubiquitous domestic feature was a distant memory.

At the end of the Middle Ages, turners did adapt their skills to produce wooden parts for new industries. Many made components for frame furniture. In particular, they made legs, stretchers, spindles and seat rails from beech, oak and ash for chairs, as they became popular. Turners also made vast quantities of pulley blocks, often from ash, for rigging on ships, and spigots used to draw beer from barrels – again, usually ash – as well as tool handles. By the end of the eighteenth century, though, bowl-turning across many parts of Europe had declined massively or disappeared altogether. Only in the remotest, rural areas of the Continent did it continue into the twentieth century.

Walking into Robin's workshop was like stepping back into the Middle Ages. Piles of wood were strewn on the floor. There were wooden stools, clubs and various tools I could not identify. A single shelf along one of the whitewashed stone walls was piled with old wooden bowls, boards and plates. At the back of the byre, where the daylight had lost its confidence, I could make out the silhouette of a woodworking bench. On a table inside the door lay dozens of long, wooden-handled

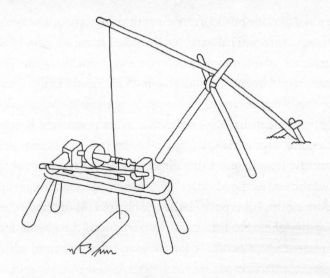

Pole lathe

chisels, which Robin called 'hook tools'. The room was dominated by the pole lathe – a simple framework of posts and beams with a 10-foot springy pole attached horizontally, above head height.

Lathes were first used for wood-turning in Europe and Asia 2,500 years ago, but this type of pole lathe was popular from around AD 500 and had its heyday in medieval Europe. It was probably developed for bowl-turning and then later adapted for turning the parts of chairs. Robin's pole was a rowan sapling, but it could just as easily have been ash, he said. The shape and size are more important than the species.

The pole was anchored at one end. From the free end, a strap ran down to a wooden foot treadle on the floor. This strap is wrapped around a spiked shaft or 'mandrel', which is knocked into the block of wood about to be turned. The turner presses the treadle down, the mandrel revolves, the block spins forward and the pole bends; release the treadle, the pole springs straight and the block spins back again. The mandrel and the block of wood rotate on two metal spikes fixed to uprights, one of which is adjustable to make sure the block is secured as it spins. As the treadle is depressed, the turner takes a cut from the wood with a hook tool, and slowly shapes the bowl.

Many different types of lathe can be used for turning wood. Wheelwrights favoured great wheel lathes for turning large elm hubs; water-powered lathes were once common across Europe, wherever steep streams ran; and steam-powered lathes, and later electric-powered lathes, released wood-turners from reliance upon the landscape and the weather. There is, though, something ascetic, holistic and even beautiful about the pole lathe, which sets it apart. I understood how it worked immediately. It is powered by human effort working in unison with the inherent spring in a sapling tree. I thought of a quote from Roy Underhill, the American woodworker and author: 'We have spent millennia devising ways to avoid this sort of physical work, and yet we always return to it. It is a part of us.'

Robin had offered to turn not just one bowl; he had gener-ously agreed to make a 'nest of bowls' from a piece of my ash – a set of three bowls, one inside the other, out of the same bowl blank, whereby the hollow of the largest bowl is cut out in a perfect hemisphere that forms the outside of the next bowl, and so on until the whole blank has been used up.

Making nests is difficult because the turner can neither see the cutting edge of the tool while it is working between bowls, nor readily gauge the thickness of each bowl: 'It's the Holy Grail of turning,' Robin said.

Robin chose a small mandrel and found the centre of the bowl blank by eye: 'There's no perfect place. There are many variables and it's a judgement,' he said, before gouging out a small piece of wood. The mandrel was then driven in with eight firm wallops of the hammer. He span the bowl blank upside down to check it, wrapped the strap around the mandrel and, with a wooden mallet, fixed it into the lathe. He pulled a hook tool off the rack and sharpened the metal cutting edge with a stone. He stood straight, inhaled a great lungful of air as if preparing to swim a length underwater, and pressed down hard on the treadle for the first time. The bowl span. The wood rasped furiously, as the metal kissed it. Tiny streaks of ash flew off and caught the light, like sparks from a Catherine wheel. In a moment that transcended the ages, the flecks floated timelessly to the floor.

'This is the first cut. I'm feeling my way into the wood and getting a sense of how it's going to turn,' Robin said. After half a minute, he looked up and flashed a smile: 'Yep, it's nice. I like it. I like your tree.'

It took a second to depress and release the treadle. The bowl blank was in almost perpetual motion, pausing momentarily at either end of its rotation as the rowan pole readied itself to straighten and bend again. Robin only drove the tool against the wood as he pressed on the treadle, but the noise of the iron cutting the wood hadn't faded away before it began again. The sound was constant and circular, rising and falling in intensity with the direction the ash blank span.

'When the tool is going down the grain, I get a much cleaner cut – a "tsss, tsss". When I'm cutting in against the grain, though, the tool has to work harder. It doesn't run smoothly and you get that real "thuw-chh",' Robin said.

Robin had told me that he carried hundreds of bowl shapes or forms in his head. While he was skimming the bumps off the outside of the blank, he was mentally searching his archive for the form that would work best in this instance. Creativity is, I was reminded, the mastery of a skill through prolonged practice. He paused briefly to show me the path the iron edge of the tool impressed in the wood: 'Here, I'm working down the grain. And here I'm going across the end grain, and then here I'm going directly against the grain. The more fibrous the wood is, the harder it is to cut against the grain. You need good technique and sharp tools.'

As the friction of the centring device began to burn into the wood, the workshop filled with the distinctive aroma of ash, a natural perfume I was becoming familiar with and growing to adore.

'Smells great, doesn't it?' Robin said, pausing to strip a layer of clothing off and turning the bowl blank around in the lathe. 'The smell of ash lingers on the tools. Not all wood smells good, you know. Elm smells awful. But ash – ah! – it's a bit like freshly cut hay. How do you bottle that?'

With a different hook tool clasped in his lean, weathered hands, Robin began to open up the inside of the first bowl.

The ash was working better than he had initially hoped. Ten minutes later, he paused again, to take another layer off. He wiped the sweat from his forehead with a finger. He had changed his mind about the shape: the grain pattern inside the bowl was very strong. He was going to make a plainer bowl – to let the grain speak for itself.

Changing tools more frequently now, Robin worked with greater care. He regularly stopped pressing the treadle and thrust his tool into the gap between the outer bowl and the now diminished inner blank. Working completely blind, around a curved surface, trying to finish a bowl to within a millimetre of thickness is a tall order, even for an accomplished turner. If the tool gets snagged, it can lever and split the bowl. The quiet moments between the spinning and scraping got longer. The wind drove the carpet of wood shavings across the floor into drifts, like snow. With the lathe stationary, Robin carefully worked the hook tool into the gap again. There was a loud 'tch-ock' as the core snapped out.

Smiling brightly, Robin released the fixings of the lathe. He ran his hands round and round the bowl and held it up to the daylight on fingertips, like a venerated chalice: 'That's good. So we've got a clean cut all the way down to the base. There's a small scar in the centre, which I'll finish off by hand. Lovely ash bowl.'

Before Kate Middleton stole the heart of a prince, the most famous person to come from Bucklebury Common in Berkshire was George William Lailey, known during his lifetime as 'the last bowl-turner'. Bucklebury Common was once the centre of a thriving community of bowl-turners: the hamlet where Lailey lived is called Turner's Green and the craft ran in his family for over 200 years.

Lailey was immortalized by the consummate journalist and popular author H. V. Morton in his bestselling travelogue, *In Search of England*, published in 1927. My dad gave me a copy of the book twenty-five years ago, when I first showed an interest in travelling and writing. The moral tone was out of date then, but the underlying ideological motive of the book remains relevant today. Morton believed that the strength of a nation like England (the series *In Search of* . . . went on to cover Wales, Scotland and several other countries) relied on the health of its rural areas. *In Search of England* reads superficially like a paean to a lost green land; underneath the chocolate box images he creates, though, Morton is insisting on the continuance of that green land.

The writer's journey begins as he drives west out of London in a Bull-nosed Morris, to Bucklebury Common. There he meets George Lailey, who 'turns bowls exactly as they did in the days of Alfred the Great . . . to say that eight hundred years seem to have stopped at the door conveys nothing. The room was an Anglo-Saxon workshop.' Lailey turned platters, trays, candlesticks, egg cups and magnificent sets of nesting bowls from elm, all on a pole lathe, using hook tools that he forged himself. There were one or two other bowl-turners still practising the craft in Britain during the 1920s, mainly in West Wales, but Morton knew he was writing history. He knew that when Lailey died, a remarkable woodworking tradition would be gone. The wealth of knowledge about wood that had accreted over generations, and which had become intuitive to bowl-turners, would disappear too. In one passage from the book, Morton questions Lailey's motives:

'You could make a lot of money if you wanted to,' I told him.

'Money?' he said with a slow, faun-like smile. 'Money's only storing up trouble, I think. I like making bowls more than I like making money.'

George Lailey died in 1958, aged eighty-nine. His lathe and tools were acquired and put on permanent display at the Museum of English Rural Life in Reading.

'That was my introduction to bowl-turning,' Robin told me. 'I saw the pole lathe in the Museum and I realized there was no one left in Britain who could work it. So I built one myself and learnt. I owe Lailey a lot. I even managed to buy a breadboard that he made. I use it every day and at sixty years old, it is better than new.'

We had left the wind cursing around Lee Farm for half an hour and gone back to Robin's house for a late lunch. We ate bread, cheese and delicious soup, but I was more enamoured by the tableware than the food. I shouldn't have been surprised but everything seemed to be made from wood – the bowls, plates, spoons, breadboards, ladle, butter dish, fruit bowl, knife-holder, cups and the stools we sat on.

Robin first obtained a job in the woods as a National Trust Warden after the famous October 1987 storm, a cataclysmic gale that flattened some 15 million trees and rearranged the woodlands of south-east England in one dramatic night. He worked for an old woodman and learnt to make fences, gates and stiles – everything the property needed, in fact – from the local timber resource. He moved on to work in Hatfield Forest, Essex, described by Dr Oliver Rackham, the eminent botanist and woodland historian, as: 'the last wooded royal Forest in England in which all components survive . . . a microcosm of English history'. There, they milled their own timber and sold it to local craftsmen, while Robin began to learn about traditional woodworking. Seventeen years ago – over forty years after Lailey retired – Robin gave up his day job, built a pole lathe from scratch and began turning bowls full-time. Determined to make a living from actually selling his wares, rather than teaching courses and doing paid demonstrations, he produced large quantities and sold them cheaply. The emphasis was on utility, not ornamentation. You might say he was going against the grain, but it worked.

'Today, there are 20,000 bowls and plates of mine out there somewhere,' Robin said, as we cleared the kitchen. 'People are eating off them every day, just like I hope you'll use your ash bowls every day.'

Halfway through turning the second bowl, Robin came across a black knot buried in the wood. Knots are the stubs of smaller, side branches that have died, usually because they were shaded out or broken off. The side branch then dies back to the surface of the trunk or main branch and the stub is subsequently encased by the growth of new wood.

There was a hint of concern: the knot might drop out, leaving a hole. Robin worked around it with great precision,

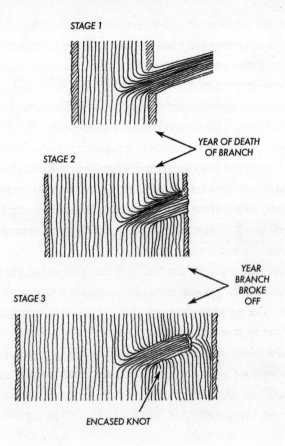

STAGE 1

YEAR OF DEATH
OF BRANCH

STAGE 2

YEAR
BRANCH
BROKE
OFF

STAGE 3

ENCASED KNOT

stopping regularly to run his fingers over the wall of the bowl: 'Nearly, nearly . . . ooh, we're in the clear,' he said.

The hardwood timber industry traditionally regards knots as defects. Because the abnormal cell structure of a knot runs at an angle to the surrounding grain direction, the wood around knots is weaker and inconsistent, affecting the strength properties of that piece of wood. As the properties of knot-free timber are more predictable, it tends to have a higher value. Thus great efforts are made in commercial forestry to grow hardwood trees that have no side branches below the living crown of the tree.

For the creative woodworker, however, knots and other irregularities of nature can be valuable features: they can form the heart of beautiful craftsmanship and art, even if they do cause problems. Robin had skilfully worked around the knot encased in my piece of ash branch wood. He had managed to convert a problem into a feature, enhancing the natural element and the beauty of the bowl. He looked content in his work again.

There was another 'tch-ock' sound. The second bowl was finished. Robin handed it to me in the doorway of the byre. I ran my finger over the knot. A circle of dark wood the size of a shirt button was recessed in the creamy wood, half an inch below the rim. A patch of brown, stained wood spread from one side of the knot. I tried to think what this patch looked like – the profile of an otter's head, perhaps. It was inaccurately mirrored further round the rim by another small pool of stained wood.

Uneven waves of grain, like contour lines on a map, swept down from the rim into the centre of the bowl from four points. In places, the grain was tight; in others, the waves swept lazily around the curves. The effect was enigmatic – as if there was a riddle in the pattern. I ran my thumb around the outside of the bowl. I could feel the impressions left by the cutting tools. In some spots, the grain was perceptibly dimpled. In one area, the surface was gnarled and pitted.

Frequently, I raised the bowl to my nose and inhaled the smell. I thought of some of the things I own that are in daily use – things made from synthetic materials like my laptop, my phone and the biros I use to take notes. I wondered if I had ever taken the trouble to smell them.

Wood has sensual powers that cannot be quantified. It may even be that these powers are the most important properties of wood today. Through odour, colour, resonance and warmth, we develop a sentimental attachment to artefacts made of wood that often reaches beyond their practical use. It is difficult to know exactly why we make these attachments, not least because our appreciation of such properties is so subjective. For some, touching wood engenders a feeling of safety; for others, it is a reminder of the proximity of nature; for yet others, it is about connecting to the past. Perhaps, for all of us, it is some kind of biological response. After all, we came down from the trees and for 99.9 per cent of our time on earth we have lived in natural environments: our physiological functions remain finely tuned to nature.

There have been plenty of studies that have attempted to better understand the power of wood: such studies have shown that in classrooms and offices with wooden furniture, blood pressure and pulse rates tend to drop – wood is thus responsible for reducing stress levels and improving quality of sleep. I read about one study, albeit a small one, that showed how the introduction of wooden artefacts, including trays, in the dining room of a care centre for the elderly improved interactions between the residents, and even increased their awareness of the surroundings.

Environmental psychology is a relatively new branch of scientific study that focuses on the relationship between the physical environment and human behaviour and well-being. It pulls together a varied and growing body of research that attempts to understand how and why spending time in the natural world might have beneficial effects on our physical and psychological health. One of the first and best-known studies, by Roger S. Ulrich thirty years ago, concluded that patients recovering from surgery in rooms with a window facing natural surroundings took less medicine for pain relief than patients with a window facing a brick wall. Further research has looked at the relationship between trees and the perception of safety in inner cities, the effect of gardening on the quality of life of people with disabilities, and how the use of wood in interiors can reduce levels of stress in schools. The effect of wood in hospitals has been studied in many countries including Finland, Norway, Austria, South Korea, Japan, USA, Canada and Denmark. The research has not been systematic and it is far from conclusive. However, observations do seem to show that humans react to wood in interiors both psychologically and physiologically, and the reaction is usually positive. The findings correspond with the increasingly impressive shelf of psychological research that says spending time in nature improves cognition, helps with anxiety and depression, and even enhances human empathy.

In Japan, *shinrin-yoku* or 'forest bathing' – essentially going for a stroll in an ancient forest – is established as a standard, modern form of preventative medicine. Inspired by ancient Shinto and Buddhist practices, nearly a quarter of the Japanese population enjoy forest bathing today. There is also a bona fide field of study that tries to understand not just why walking in a fragrant, old growth forest is good for us, but also how the magic of trees works on humans at a molecular level, in our cells and neurons. The research data is compelling: leisurely forest walks reduce heart rate and blood pressure, decrease sympathetic nerve activity and lower levels of the stress hormone, cortisol.

Throughout my adult life, I have suffered from mild depression. It has never been an insuperable problem. It comes in bouts, often arriving when I don't expect it. I endure a week or two of anxiety and self-loathing, which makes working impossible. It also places a huge strain on my family. Then it goes. Since I moved to the Black Mountains in Wales, where I live now, I have engineered spending time in the woods into my life and I suffer from depression noticeably less. In the same way, being in the woods helped me through my grief when my dad died a few years ago.

I manage the small piece of woodland around my house. I work in other woods, as part of the local community woodland group. I have built a wooden cabin among the alder, oak and beech at the bottom of my property, beside the stream – this is my office. I am not assuming I will never suffer from depression again. Nor am I saying that the only way to keep the 'black dog' off my back is to spend time among the trees. I am merely observing that my personal experience of 'forest bathing' has been good for my well-being. The whole project with this ash tree has been positive too.

I let my fingers explore the concave interior of the bowl

again. The grain ran down in semi-circles, like ripples retreating from a rock dropped into a pond. I rubbed my thumb across the rough grain to find the small, smooth knot. Having my cereal out of an ash bowl – I'll take that over Prozac any day, I thought.

Robin held the two finished bowls together, carefully inspecting the rims to check they were in proportion. If you set yourself the task of making a nest, you want the bowls to look like they belong together, he explained. They did. He walked to the door to admire them in stronger light and nodded approvingly. Placing them on the bench inside each other, he said: 'I'm getting a feel for how this ash tools.'

Having selected a new hook tool to make the final bowl, he began sharpening the metal point. He had recently been turning beech, and every time you change species, he explained, all the cutting edges have to be reset, because each species cuts slightly differently. For this reason, Robin would normally buy an entire tree, or several trees of the same species, and work his way through the batch. He applied the sharpening stone to the iron hook again and whistled, mimicking the call of the curlew coming again off the hill.

'It's good to work with different woods,' Robin said, 'although it's also good to get into a batch of the same timber. It may be fiddly and slow making the first bowl with a new tree, but you get familiar with the progression of the tools. By the tenth bowl, I'm flying.'

I counted thirty hook tools in a rack on the workbench. There were as many again, standing in troops on the floor beneath. Together, they could have comprised the armoury of a warlike Iron Age tribe or the apparatus of a ghoulish dentist from a Gothic fantasy. Each tool comprised a 2-foot piece of straight wood with a foot-long, iron spike secured in one end. Some of the wooden handles were de-barked and crudely fashioned with an axe. A few had grooves cut into the wood to aid grip, and a couple were bound with strips of sweat-weathered gaffer tape. The iron cutting edges, the business end of the tools, were all subtly different. Some were shaped like leaflets, 3 inches long, curved and narrowing to a point. Others curled at the end, like Hart's-tongue ferns waiting to unfurl and straighten in spring. Instinctively, I knew these tools would not function well in another turner's hands. They were all adjusted in shape, feel, temper, weight – and even character – to their owner. There was a unity of disposition between the tools and Robin – the legacy of years of common service.

'I forged all these tools myself and I know them intimately. They don't have names. A tool only needs a name if you're trying to sell it, but I know exactly what each one does. I know how long ago I made it and I know its history. I have a feel for how many times I've sharpened each one. This one here is my current favourite,' Robin said, raising one of the implements off the rack and thrusting it towards me. More than half the metal had been sharpened away.

'Bearing in mind I sharpen it with a little stone, by hand – that adds up to a lot of sharpening. Having got it to this stage, there's very little metal to act as resistance. When it goes through the wood, it cuts very, very efficiently. But they don't last for ever. They all have a lifespan – fifteen years or so. It'll not be long before this one breaks.'

The remaining bowl blank was just 4½ inches in diameter, half the size of the original. Robin fixed it into the lathe and began pumping the treadle again, like a guitarist extravagantly tapping out a heavy, funk baseline.

A group of men in gaiters and raincoats stopped outside the workshop and peered in. We all exchanged breezy greetings. Robin swiped another finger of sweat off his brow and pressed on the treadle. White sparks of ash flew through the air.

'Well, that's a traditional way of doing things,' one of the walkers said, wide-eyed, before they all rustled off down the track.

'Tch-ock' – the third bowl was finished. Robin perched on a bench and scraped off the scars on the inside of all three bowls. He used a double-handed tool with a long, curved metal cutting edge – one of his oldest tools, forged out of an old car spring eighteen years ago. The first cuts took off large flecks of wood, but the strokes got progressively lighter, until he exerted the force you might use to strike a match.

'It's like cleaning a navel,' he said, looking up for a moment with bright, eager eyes. 'Again, feel is more important than anything else. After each cut, I feel the surface of the wood with my hand. That tells me more than my eyes.'

To finish, Robin put his mark – three small notches – on the flat bottom of each bowl. At home, later, he would treat them with raw, cold-pressed linseed oil. For now, though, his work was done. He arranged the bowls together, carefully matching up the grain to highlight how the patterns ran through them all, like the swell of the sea pressing into a cove. The bowls were roughly 8½, 6½ and 4½ inches in diameter. They mirrored each other in delightful, inexact symmetry. They were light, but sturdy. They were ultimately utilitarian – that they were also beautiful was coincidental. The bowls embodied not just Robin's skill as a turner, but his idealism too. They had character and life; somehow they resonated with the spirit of growth and the aspiration of my ash tree. I wondered if there was a more elemental possession that a person could have.

Robin expressed genuine delight at how the bowls had turned out – not for me, nor my venture, but for himself. They could have been the first bowls he had ever turned. Then again, you could say they were: every piece of wood is different, and there must be a constant sense of renewal in what Robin does, day after day.

'These bowls will evolve. They'll change shape a bit and develop their own patina as they dry. They'll get nicer and nicer the more you use them,' he said.

I promised Robin I would use them every day: I'll eat like a king, albeit a medieval one. Looking out of the byre, we suddenly realized the afternoon had vanished. Robin shut up the workshop. We set off down the valley in the dying light, towards the pub.

CHAPTER 5

The Devil's Finger

'Dark is the colour of the ash;
timber that makes the wheels to go;
Rods he furnishes for horsemen's hands,
his form turns battle into flight.'
'Song of the Forest Trees',
traditional Irish verse

Common ash grows almost everywhere in Britain. I started to see it all over the land – in hedgerows, in copses on village boundaries, standing in fields, in ravines, near ancient fortifications, beside rivers and streams, alone on limestone moorlands, in old quarries, near ponds, beside abandoned farmsteads on dead-end lanes, in parks and peeking out of the roofs of woodlands.

On my bicycle in winter, I picked out the silhouettes of solitary ash trees on distant ridges; I saw congregations of ash saplings in clearings on woodland walks in spring; from trains, I glimpsed yellow spots in faraway woods and knew the ash leaves were signalling the onset of autumn. Landscapes I knew well shone with fresh meaning. Landscapes I had never seen before radiated with ash like illuminated medieval manuscripts. I mentioned this to my wife, who studied history of art: she told me how the ash tree has figured highly in the

British landscape-painting tradition, from Constable (the ash was his favourite tree) to David Hockney.

One day when I was out on my bicycle, I pedalled through a tiny village called Cross Ash. Then I started to notice how the word 'ash' figures in lots of place-names. British place-names are linguistic fossils, coined by our ancestors a thousand years ago or more, as living units of speech, to describe a place in terms of its topography, appearance, use or ownership. Sometimes they simply referenced the species of tree that grew there.

I looked in the dog-eared road atlas that lives under the seat in our car. I scanned through an old British *Gazeteer* or geographical dictionary that I, for reasons I can't remember, bought in a second-hand bookshop years ago. I ended up scouring the Oxford *Dictionary of British Place Names* in my local library. My list of places related to the ash tree grew and grew: Ashmanhaugh, Ashenhurst, Ashurst Wood, Beggars Ash, Mark Ash, Whitnash, Weobley Ash, Ashwater, Ashwicken, Askam-in-Furness, Askern, Ashby cum Fenby, Ashby Puerorum, Ashby Folville, Ashley Green and Ashby-de-la-Zouch. The word is braided into the landscape, just as the roots of the trees themselves are woven into the earth. No other tree species, not even oak or birch, is so commonly referenced. Ash-related place-names are extant from Inverness to Cornwall and Cumbria to Essex. In Thomas Hardy's *Tess of the d'Urbervilles*, Tess finds work in Flintcomb-Ash.

'Ash', as in Ash, Kent, Ash, Surrey, or Ash Magna in Shropshire simply means 'place at the ash tree'. Ashampstead means 'homestead by the ash trees'. Ashbourne means 'stream where the ash trees grow'; Ashburnham – 'meadow by the stream where the ash trees grow'; Ashburton – 'farmstead by the stream where the ash trees grow'; and Ashbury – 'stronghold where the ash trees grow'. Ashby, a common component of place-names in the north and Midlands of England, means 'farmstead or village where ash trees grow'. Ashley – again, there are several – means 'ash tree wood or clearing'. Ashmore is a 'pool where ash trees grow', and Ashendon means 'place overgrown with ash trees'. Ashfield needs no translation.

Ashton, as in Ashton Keynes, West Ashton, Steeple Ashton, Ashton upon Mersey and Lower Ashton, means 'farmstead by the ash trees'. Ashwell marks a 'spring where ash trees grow', Askrigg is 'ash tree ridge', and Askwith is simply 'ash tree wood'. Aspatria is the 'ash tree of St Patrick', the patron saint of Ireland. Incidentally, popular legend credits St Patrick with driving all the snakes out of Ireland in the fifth century, for which task he brandished an ash stick.

Slightly harder to interpret are the place-names with 'esh' as an element: 'esh' like 'ash' is thought to derive from the Old English word for *Fraxinus excelsior*, *'aesc'*. So, Esher probably means 'district where ash trees grow', and Eshton is a 'farmstead by the ash trees'. The word for ash in Welsh is *'onnen'*: again, it is common in place-names, just as *'fuinseóg'* – ash in the Gaelic language, Irish – is common across the green fields of Ireland. Around the north-west coast of the British Isles, where Viking place-names are common, 'eski', as in Eskdale, is a prefix that means 'place where ash trees grow'.

Once I had exhausted British place-names, I looked abroad. Ash grows almost everywhere in France, except in the high mountains. The French word for ash – '*frêne*' – appears across the nation in places like Fresnes, Freneuse, Saint-Martin-du-Frêne, Le-Champ-du-Frêne, Notre-Dame-du-Frêne, Frêne-de-Chassy, Les Villeneuve-aux-Frênes and Le Beau Frêne, while simply Le Frêne is a common name for farmsteads. Further east and north, '*frêne*' gives way to the German word for ash, '*Esche*', as in Eschbourg in Alsace and Esch-sur-Alzette, the second town of Luxembourg. By this time, I was not surprised to discover that 'Esch' is a common component of place-names in Germany.

I then wondered if the tree had made such a bold impression on place-names in the USA. Of course it had: the tree was just too useful to go unnoticed. 'Ashland' is one of the most common place-names in the USA, according to the exhaustive list held by the Geographic Names Information System. Around 400 different populated places have 'ash' as a component in their name, from Ashby, Alabama, to Ash Ridge, Ohio and Ashwood, Virginia, to Ash Fork, Arizona. There are twenty-one places called Ashton, seventeen called Ashley and nine simply called Ash. Even the Spanish word for ash gets a look in, as in Fresno, California.

In Britain, ash does not just grow everywhere; significantly, it will also grow fast in the right circumstances. In fact, ash is one of the most productive hardwoods we have. On the best sites, in woodlands formed on moist, lime-rich soil, ash yields more than all other hardwoods with the exception of beech. The volume of timber produced can be as much as 10m³ per hectare per year – a huge amount – though the average is more typically 4 to 6m³ per hectare per year. Ash trees grow fast for the first forty to sixty years: this is a common rotation age for commercially grown ash in the modern era. For much of history, though, ash trees would have been felled and used before they reached this age.

Ash is highly productive both when it is coppiced – the practice of cutting the tree back to ground level, to encourage regrowth – and when it is pollarded – cutting the crown back to the top of the trunk. Ash trees also mature early: a pole just 6 inches in diameter is as valuable and durable as the timber from a much larger tree. As Sir Herbert Maxwell wrote in *Trees: A Woodland Notebook*, published in 1915: 'The properties which ensure to the ash . . . this superiority to all rivals are its hardihood, the matchless quality of its timber for many purposes, and its market value from a very early age.'

Another important silvicultural characteristic of ash is that the species is capable of prolific natural regeneration. Today, it is the largest contributor to natural regeneration in British broad-leaved woodlands, accounting for more than 40 per cent of all observed seedlings and saplings in some surveys. In the small patch of woodland beside my house, there are several hundred self-seeded ash saplings. More thorough studies have found ash regeneration can achieve densities of 150,000 seedlings per hectare on ideal sites, though only a small number of these eventually grow into trees. Like oak, birch and sycamore, ash is also a 'pioneer' species: it is quick to seed and grow in vacant ground. The consequences of these characteristics – wide distribution, good growth rates and profuse natural regeneration – are significant. Ash timber has always been readily available.

*

'Ash has many qualities that make it ideal for arrow shafts, but the fact that it grows almost everywhere and it grows like mad has to be significant,' Tom Mareschall said, taking the first bundle of wood out of my arms. He was broad and stout with a pate of white hair and a closely cropped beard. A tattoo curled out beneath a grey T-shirt sleeve on his hulking upper-right arm. As you might expect of an artisan bowyer, arrow-maker and blacksmith, he had powerful hands with great, meaty fingers. He spoke with a deep voice, from the corner of his mouth. There was a hint of an Essex brogue and a tiny glint of menace in his dark, heavily set eyes. If it all kicked off, I thought, he was a man you would want by your side.

When we had finished unloading my car, I glanced around the workshop, a brick shed beside a farm in undulating Essex countryside. A dozen bows in various shapes and lengths, from 6-foot longbows down to kids' hunting bows, lay on racks across the window. Yew bow blanks and half-worked yew bows leant against the whitewashed walls in gangs.

I had brought 130 arrow blanks, oblong sticks measuring $\frac{9}{16}$ inch x $\frac{9}{16}$ inch x 31 inches, all sawn from a single plank from near the outside of the trunk of my tree. In return for the wood, Tom had agreed to show me how to make a medieval arrow, in as near a traditional way as he could. Tom put the kettle on and began inspecting the wood.

'In the Middle Ages, some arrow shafts were just peeled sticks – perfectly serviceable for hunting and, of course, cheap. The timber for good arrows, however, would have always been cleaved and ash cleaves very well. Your timber has been sawn but that doesn't matter because it's straight-grained and clean. It looks good,' Tom said.

He placed one of my oblong sticks of ash on a shooting board, a piece of flat wood with a recess in the surface, blocked at one end. With a hand plane, he leant over the table and began to shave off the long edges. Ringlets gathered at the end of the board in a pile. Tom was already warming up. He stood straight, took a slurp of coffee and held the ash stick up. It was now octagonal. He placed it back in the shooting blank and repeated the process, shaving the eight edges off. Curl by curl the square stick was transformed into a round shaft. He held it up to eye level and squinted at it. 'We've now got an approximately round shaft. Not bad, actually. You can see the grain clearly. Nice and straight. This'll make a decent arrow. Feel it, it's got a bit of weight to it,' Tom said.

For tens of thousands of years, humans have fashioned innumerable different species of wood into shafted projectiles. During the late Middle Ages, though, when the longbow reached the apogee of its prowess as the deadliest weapon in European warfare, and the aerodynamic design and technology of arrows reached a fearsome pinnacle, then the favoured wood for making arrows was ash.

We happen to know most of the best 'livery' or army-issue arrows were made from ash during this period, and particularly during the Hundred Years War (1337–1453) with France, because of contemporary records. Documents like the Exchequer Rolls give details of the arms and ammunition, including the number of sheaths of ash shafts with goose feathers and the barrels of arrowheads, delivered to the national armoury in the Tower of London.

Even though it was easy to obtain, ash was also favoured for other reasons, Tom explained. As a relatively dense wood, ash is a good compromise in the matter of weight. It is light enough to shoot a long distance, yet heavy enough to maintain its high, initial velocity and cause damage when it reaches the target: 'Just the thing for piercing armour or skewering a French knight to his horse at 200 yards,' Tom said.

The Elizabethan scholar Roger Ascham, author of the great Tudor treatise on archery, *Toxophilus*, published in 1545, understood this. He wrote: 'Yet, as concerning sheaffe arrowes for war (as I suppose) it were better to make them of good Ashe . . . For all other woodes that ever I proved, Ashe being bigge is swiftest, and againe hevye to geve a great stripe withal.'

To be shot accurately as well as a long way, however, the wooden shaft of an arrow needs other properties. Importantly, it must be stiff enough to resist the force of being shot. 'Stiffness' is, in materials science, the property of a structure, an arrow shaft in this case. As the arrow is being compressed by the bowstring when it is shot, we are interested in what is called 'axial stiffness', that is stiffness along the length of the arrow. This can be calculated by multiplying the cross-sectional area by the modulus of elasticity of the piece of wood and dividing by the length of the shaft.

Archers and bowyers sometimes refer to stiffness as 'dynamic spine', though they are not exactly the same thing.

Dynamic spine is determined by the shaft length, the weight of the head and the stiffness of the centre point of the shaft when it is static. It is important: if the dynamic spine of an arrow is correct the arrow can withstand the initial impulse of release, and leave the bow cleanly. If it is wrong, the arrow will make contact in unpredictable ways with the bow as it is shot, reducing accuracy.

Less powerful bows require arrows with less dynamic spine, because they deform the arrow less as it is accelerated. Conversely, powerful bows need stiffer arrows with greater dynamic spine. The longbows, or 'great warbows' as they are called, associated with the age of English military greatness during the late Middle Ages were very powerful. I had already tried to draw one of Tom's yew bows, a replica of a sixteenth-century longbow. I had got nowhere. Tom told me that there were only a dozen or so people in the country capable of drawing and firing it accurately today. The 'draw weight', that is the force required to draw the string, of a typical longbow from this period is disputed, but it was somewhere between 90 and 160 pounds-force. That is equivalent to picking that weight up off the ground, and holding it out on a straight arm. Hunting bows, by comparison, commonly had draw weights of 50 to 60 pounds-force. An arrow shaft required a great deal of dynamic spine to withstand the force of being shot from a medieval warbow: ash provided it.

'I have this image of a medieval archer – rough, grizzled, largely uneducated but smart. They had to be to survive. The enormous strength they gained by training with the bow from childhood gave them advantages, not least in their sheer physical presence. Imagine a broad, barrel-chested man, bulky and powerful, a bit like a rugby back row forward. Life at home for these archers was one of drudgery and poverty. They were generally yeomen and foresters – men who had often grown up close to the land, with a bow and arrow in their hands. Then there is this opportunity to take your bow and go to France and fight, and if you're lucky enough to survive, make a bit of money. I mean, what an adventure. In many ways, it's something I'd quite like to do now: take my bow and arrows and my skills, off we go and just see how we get on,' Tom said.

Like a medieval archer, Tom grew up with a bow and arrow in his hands. He made his first bow from bamboo sticks aged seven. Suffering from Asperger's syndrome (though undiagnosed), he played truant from school for several years from the age of nine and got his education instead from the woods. As a teenager, Tom was taught how to make longbows exactly as they were made 600 years ago, by a local estate gardener and keen artisan bowyer. He learnt the art of drawing the bow round the body, developing calluses on two fingers on his right hand. He learnt about the battles of Halidon Hill, Crécy, Poitiers and Agincourt. He was hooked. When Tom was fifteen, his mentor died, and he inherited an entire bow-making workshop.

Today, Tom makes bows and arrows for half of the year. For the other half, he runs bow-making courses, teaches archery master classes and provides demonstrations and talks. During the summer, he travels around Britain introducing young people to archery and medieval military history, which he is passionate about.

Tom secured the now rounded shaft of ash vertically through a hole in the workbench. With a tile saw, he cut a 2-inch split, parallel to the grain, through the centre of the tail of the shaft. 'I'm creating the nock, where the bowstring sits, and I'll reinforce it with a piece of buffalo horn. Traditionally, they would have used cow horn, but since the BSE issue, abattoirs can't sell it to us. The horn has been soaked in water and flattened. I just have to trim it now, so it fits snugly into the slot. The bone stops the arrow from splitting under the force of the bowstring,' he explained.

He lit a ring on the gas stove and stood a tin of glue inside a pan of water. The glue was made from cured, desiccated rabbit skin. A natural glue, it is prone to rot: Tom added a few flecks of verdigris by scratching the green coating off a piece of copper with a scalpel. When the glue was ready, he coated the bone and secured it inside the split in the shaft, working quickly. The bone was trimmed to length. With a piece of sandpaper (the skin of a dog fish would have traditionally been used), he finished the nock. His two fingers sat comfortably around the tail of the shaft, dead on the bowstring. The arrow was taking shape.

Edward I, an accomplished general when he became King of England in 1272, was arguably the first monarch to fully appreciate the military capabilities of the longbow. Campaigning in Wales in the 1280s, Welsh longbowmen took a heavy toll on Edward's army, convincing him of the need to have them within his own ranks. Between around 1300 and 1550, the longbow was the standard infantry weapon in the English army.

During this period, archery was as commonplace a pastime as football is today. In the fourteenth century, archery practice on Sundays was made compulsory for able-bodied men and boys aged from eight to sixty, by a series of royal decrees. On feast days, tournaments with prizes were held, as a means for sheriffs to assess the competence of the archers within their community. Most towns and villages had an archery butt, often in a field beside the churchyard. To this day, many villages in England and Wales still have a place called 'butt field'. When I was growing up, I played rugby at a ground called The Butts. Tom told me that at the back door of the church of St Edward, King and Martyr, next to Corfe Castle in Dorset, there are marks in the walls where the archers used to sharpen their arrows before practice, 500 or more years ago. The object of enforced practice was to develop and maintain a national pool of accomplished archers who were ready for military service at any time. It worked. During the Hundred Years War, the English military was able to call upon a large cadre of fit, strong, well-trained bowmen all firing technologically advanced arrows from powerful longbows.

The effectiveness of these archers, of course, depended on a good supply of quality bows and arrows. In 1356, the Crown ordered 240,000 'good arrows' and 24,000 'best arrows' to be sent to the Tower of London. In the spring of 1415, as Henry V was preparing for the campaign that would end at Agincourt, the Keeper of the King's Wardrobe took delivery of three million arrows, each one 'split planed, fletched and bound'. Crown agents were continually in the shires, compelling the bowyers and fletchers (the traditional word for arrow-makers) to prioritize military supplies. The demands of war meant the bow- and arrow-making guilds flourished – Bowyer Row is adjacent to St Paul's Cathedral in London – and these guilds issued endless ordinances, to maintain quality in production. Between 1300 and 1500, the production of bows and arrows was a huge industry, probably one of the major industries in Britain, employing thousands.

The tactics employed by Edward III, and later Henry V, during the Hundred Years War – positioning heavily armed soldiers on foot alongside archers, in defensive set battles – proved devastating against the feudal cavalry of the Valois kings of France. These tactics lead to famous, against-the-odds victories. The names of these battles still trip off the tongues of English schoolchildren, six centuries later – Agincourt, Poitiers and, perhaps the engagement most indelibly linked to the prowess of archers, Crécy.

'At whatever hour you approach you will find us ready to meet you in the fields, with God's help, which thing we desire above all else,' Edward III wrote to King Philip VI of France, on the eve of the battle of Crécy in August 1346. The taunt worked. Edward had most likely reconnoitred the battlefield in advance, as it provided an excellent defensive position and elevation for his retinue of 5,000 or so archers. In the first exchanges, the English archers 'poured out their arrows . . . so thickly and evenly that they fell like snow', Froissart, the French chronicler, wrote. In the fear and confusion of the arrow-storm, the lack of French tactical forethought was exposed. The arrow-storms were a deadly and effective preliminary. The engagement would later hinge on the ability of the heavily outnumbered, dismounted English knights and foot soldiers to hold their ground in the mêlée, against wave after wave of French cavalry in the moonlight. The arrows, though, had done the damage before the sun set.

The scale of the defeat was unprecedented and shocking. Reliable figures from medieval battles are notoriously hard to come by, but the consensus is around fifty English and 16,500 French dead. The King of France was wounded in the face by an arrow, and taken prisoner. The flower of French aristocracy perished. France was knee-capped as a military power for twenty years.

Firing at full tilt, the English archers could unleash twelve arrows a minute: with 5,000 archers on the field, that is 60,000 arrows 'going down the other end', as Tom put it, every sixty seconds. The best archers had three arrows in the air at any one time. The air sang with volley after volley of ash. Winston Churchill wrote of Crécy in his *History of the English-Speaking Peoples*: 'At two hundred and fifty yards the arrow hail produced effects never reached again by infantry missiles at such a range until the American Civil War.' It is no wonder the arrow was nicknamed 'the Devil's finger'.

Tom wiped the ash shavings onto the floor and placed a dozen white feathers side by side on the bench. They were large flight or 'primary' feathers from grey geese, regarded as the best arrow fletchings. Peacock and swan feathers are good alternatives. In the Middle Ages, a fletcher took only two feathers from a bird's wing at a time, Tom explained; that way, they regrow and you can pluck the same feathers again the following year.

'These feathers are all from the same wing and they have the same natural twist. An arrow is an aerofoil and with feathers from the same wing, the arrow flies true. If we put left and right wing feathers on the same arrow, however, it doesn't fly true. It oscillates and falls out of the sky,' Tom said, turning the feathers over and inspecting them carefully. 'These are all right-wing feathers, because I'm a right-handed fletcher. The grain of left-wing feathers goes the wrong way for me, making it much harder to bind them to the shaft properly. So you can tell if a fletcher was right- or left-handed, just by looking at the feathers on an arrow. This part of the process hasn't changed in millennia. It's a really fiddly job.'

Tom chose the three best feathers. With a scalpel, he trimmed the side of each feather and then split the quill down the middle, from top to bottom. With sandpaper, he flattened the split quills so they lay true on the ash shaft. He coated the tail of the shaft with rabbit glue and, working with great concentration and haste now, he placed the first feather – the 'cock feather' – at 90 degrees to the nock. Deftly, he made a loop with a thread of Belgian linen and fastened the tip of the first quill to the shaft. The next feather was similarly placed, 120 degrees further around the shaft, and bound. Holding the first two feathers in place with his fingers, he lay the third feather another 120 degrees around, equidistant between the first two. Clearly it was a job that required four or five hands. Taking care not to damage the veins of the feathers, Tom wound the linen thread around the shaft, each circle a quarter of an inch apart, to the tail of the arrow, where he tied and fastened an overhead whip knot.

While the glue was drying, Tom put the kettle on and lifted a few bows down from the racks on the wall. His best bow, the one I had already tried and failed to draw, was made of yew, the wood of choice for longbows over millennia. I had read about the Rotten Bottom bow, a yew bow pulled out of a peat bog in the Tweedsmuir Hills near the border between England and Scotland and dated by radiocarbon analysis to 4040–3640 BC. During the Middle Ages, when the hunting bow was adapted to the 'warbow' by the English military and used to devastating effect, yew was still favoured because of its high compressive strength, light weight and elasticity: an arrow shot from a traditional 'self bow', made from a single stave of yew, like the one Tom was holding, can penetrate over an inch of solid oak at 200 metres, and penetrate plate armour at 100 metres. Yew for making longbows, however, has always been hard to come by, not least because the best timber is grown slowly, at elevation and in dry regions.

At times of war during the Middle Ages, English bowyers were producing 30,000 bows a year. Most of the yew used to make bows in Britain was imported from Spain, the Adriatic and the Baltic, often at great cost. Supply was an intermittent problem over the centuries. Inevitably, alternative species were used when yew could not be obtained. Welsh bowyers commonly used wych elm. In England, bowyers were periodically required by law to make four bows of elm, wych hazel or ash to each one of yew, to ease the demand for the best yew. Also, the majority of bows – hunting bows, bows for archery practice and children's bows, for example – did not need to penetrate plate armour. More importantly, since not possessing a bow was periodically a finable offence for men, they needed to be widely available and cheap.

'A high proportion of bows throughout history would have been made from ash, just like this one,' Tom said, handing me a 6-foot weapon of smooth, lightly curved, brown ash. I recalled a drawing I'd seen of an ash bow discovered in the tomb of the Egyptian pharaoh Tutankhamun, dating from the second millennium BC. 'Shooting a yew warbow took a lifetime of training, just to develop the strength to get maximum power from it. I take this ash bow round the shows in the summer, though, and all the kids have a go with it. It's easy to draw. When I'm teaching bow-making courses, we always use ash too, because it's so much easier to work. I wouldn't want to go into battle with an ash bow, but it's perfectly serviceable and would have been very common, not least because ash was always so widely available.'

The availability and the properties of ash that made it ideal for arrows and good enough for a high proportion of bows meant the timber had other military applications too. In fact, ash was typically planted around castles across Europe during the Middle Ages. The timber was fashioned into helves for battle axes and shield handles, partly because it wears smoothly and does not readily splinter. Before that, ash was the timber of choice for spears.

In Homer's epic *The Iliad*, Achilles' spear or javelin is made of ash. It was originally a wedding gift from the gods to Achilles' parents: when 'the handsomest and bravest of all the Greeks' reached manhood, the spear was handed down. The shaft was cut from a tree on the summit of Mount Pelion and polished by the goddess Athene. Achilles achieved great fame throwing this weapon. The ash spear became an extension of Achilles and a symbol of his essence, because only he could lift it. Achilles used the ash spear to kill Hector at the climax of the Trojan War. On Achilles' death, the spear became a talisman, which allowed entrance and exit to and from the Underworld.

Both Odin, the foremost god in Scandinavian mythology, and Thor, the god of Thunder, were said to have magical spears made of ash. The lances and spears used by horsemen and infantry in the Roman Army had heads of steel and staves of seasoned ash. Contemporary writers of Latin verse often used the Latin word for ash – '*fraxinus*' – in place of 'lance' or 'spear'. As long ago as the first century AD, foresters in Britain selected the best ash as timber for the shafts of spears. The *Oxford English Dictionary* cites a now obsolete definition of 'ash', in which it means 'spear'. In J. R. R. Tolkein's *The Lord of the Rings*, the Riders of Rohan carry spears made out of ash.

At the battle of Bannockburn in 1314, the Scots were heavily armed with ash spears. Robert Bruce's men were dug into pits to protect them from the numerically superior English cavalry. When the English fell back from the ash spears in confusion, Edward II was forced to flee. The victory reaffirmed the independence of Scotland. A century later, James I, the King of Scotland, enacted a statute that required every landowner to plant and maintain ash trees in numerical proportion to their holdings. James had previously been on campaign in France with Henry V, and the law may have been prompted by his appreciation of the diverse military applications of the ash tree. James VI re-enacted the statute in 1573. The effect of this legislation may still be traced in many parts of lowland Scotland, where old ash trees are frequently found standing near farms and other homesteads.

At a time when the longbow became the pre-eminent military weapon in Britain, the crossbow was the favoured weapon on the Continent. The bows of early crossbows, called 'prods' or 'laths', were made from a single piece of wood, usually ash or yew. The bolts or 'quarrels' the crossbows shot commonly had ash shafts too.

The longbow and the crossbow became militarily obsolete at the end of the sixteenth century, ushering in a new era of European warfare involving elementary canons and muskets. The long association between ash and weaponry did not end here, though. The spear or lance, used continuously from the time of Achilles through to the fourteenth century, was revived in the form of the pike, a 15-foot-long, tapered and balanced pole weapon used by infantry in the seventeenth century. In the English Civil War, battalions of musketeers and pikemen were formed. During the Continental wars of what has been called the 'pike and shot' military era, the renowned armies of Swiss and German mercenaries became expert in the use of the 'halberd', a variation of the pike comprising an ash pole with a steel blade on the end. The pike was never meant to be thrown: it was, instead, used by infantry for attacking foot soldiers and repelling cavalry charges. The wooden pike shaft, fixed to an iron or steel spearhead, was most commonly made from seasoned ash.

'We want to put a killing machine on the end of this ash shaft, then,' Tom said, rubbing his cupped hands together. With a hand plane, he trimmed the tip of the shaft, reducing the diameter to fit inside the socket of the arrowhead. He examined it carefully after every few rasps, until he was happy with the shape.

The design of the arrowheads, he explained, developed over centuries as the blacksmith's craft improved and the needs of archers changed. There were different arrowheads for hunting birds, hunting beasts, archery practice and going to war. In the early part of the medieval period, when armour was made of leather, heavy fabric and mail, the arrowheads were long and slender. When knights began to wear plate armour, the heads were shortened into heavier, thicker, tetrahedral, bodkin-tipped devices similar to the one Tom presented to me in his hand: a 4-inch long, pointed piece of steel with real menace, the like of which turned the sky black at Crécy. There was clearly only one application for it – war. If you shot a deer with this arrowhead, it would go straight through the beast. It was designed to pierce mail and armour plate. I held the head to the shaft of the arrow: instantly, the stick of ash with goose feathers – a child's toy, from *Swallows and Amazons*, perhaps – was transformed into a murderous weapon.

Tom is also an experienced blacksmith and he hand-forges

his own arrow tips. He showed me a lump of iron ore, dug out of the earth, and explained how it is roasted in a furnace called a bloomery, with charcoal and limestone, for two weeks. The residual 'bloom' is then heated in a forge and hammered, to drive out the remaining impurities, leaving iron. To convert the iron to steel, it is baked again in a clay box with charcoal, for forty-eight hours. The blister steel is finally shaped into an arrowhead on an anvil in the forge.

Tom put a large dab of glue inside the socket of the bodkin and painted the tip of the shaft. He thrust the arrowhead onto the ash and pressed hard. He held the arrow by the tip and the nock and lifted it to his cheek, like he was taking aim with a rifle. He closed one eye and rolled the arrow around in his fingers several times. He placed the steel point on the workbench and held the arrow upright with a finger on the tail. One corner of his mouth curled upwards, hinting at a smile. Light from the window flicked across his eyes as he turned to face me. 'There you go. That's a very nice arrow. I'd shoot it. It's authentic. Yours to take home with you – one killing arrow. I really enjoyed making that,' he said. He looked sorry to be giving it away.

Tom had turned an innocuous stick of ash into an efficient and terrible weapon, capable of slaying almost anything that walked the earth. He rubbed a smear of beeswax up and down the shaft, to keep the moisture out and to bring up the grain. He painted a final coat of rabbit-skin glue over the neatly spaced rings of linen. It seemed unnecessary to take such care finishing an item with such overtly brutal purpose, but there was an aesthetic quality to the arrow too: the gentle tapering of the shaft, the delicacy of the feathers at one end and the weighted intent of the steel point at the other, connected by the straight grain of my ash wood, together amounted to a form of elegance. The arrow was so clearly handmade; that was part of the attraction too. The three feathers were uneven, the shaft was not quite perfectly round and the arrowhead bore numerous hammer marks. Just to hold the arrow was to be transported back through centuries to the Middle Ages, a time when, I couldn't help but think, Tom would have been happy to live.

CHAPTER 6

I See You Baby, Shakin' That Ash

'For runners, the rings of growth of the tree
should be as far apart as possible: that is to say, they
should be fast growing. Ash with narrow rings
breaks. There is ash and ash.'

Apsley Cherry-Garrard,
The Worst Journey in the World

A year had passed since I had felled my tree. A great deal of
my timber had been delivered to a myriad of craftsmen and
the products of their endeavours had filtered slowly back into
my house. At first, my three children showed an interest: Scarlett, aged eleven, loved eating her cereal from one of the bowls;
Lucas, fourteen, was enamoured by the bodkin-tipped arrow;
while Katrina, ten, was adamant that I use the ash pegs when
we put my old canvas tent up in the garden on a sweltering
weekend at the end of summer. They all enthusiastically
invited any visitors to the house to admire the grain in the
new kitchen worktop, but then their interest waned. Ash panelling went up on the walls of my office: it was barely
acknowledged. Benches were fitted in our back room: 'More
ash,' they groaned. I even heard Katrina whisper to a neighbour who'd come to blag some firewood: 'Don't take the ash
logs. Dad's a bit weird about them.'

'Why don't you make something out of the ash for the children?' my wife suggested. Great idea, I thought, but what? The answer came from my mum. She reminded me of the hours of finger-throbbing, sock-soaked, skull-numbing joy my brother and I had often experienced in the half-light of a winter's day on our wooden toboggan. Perfect.

'We do make sleds and luges for Olympic athletes, and we have customers from all over the world for these, but most of our business is making toboggans for recreation and amateur racing in the Alps. Here in Austria, almost every house will have a toboggan, but they last a long time. We have customers with fifty-year-old toboggans, which they bring back to us for repairs. They are like heirlooms. Our company philosophy has always been to make a quality product at a fair price, and that quality starts with good ash,' Christian Gasser told me, while making coffee. I had travelled from the UK to Austria on an overnight train, sharing a sleeper carriage from Paris to Munich with five students who had just finished their exams. I needed coffee.

'We are well known in this business because we have been making toboggans for so long. We are a small company with eight employees, but we are healthy and busy all year round,' Christian said, pouring the coffee. He was short, sinewy, square-shouldered, strong and full of energy. His youthful eyes never rested.

Johann Isser, Christian's great-great-uncle set up in business as a wheelwright in 1909 outside the small town of Mattrei, beside the road over the Alps from Innsbruck in Austria to

Bolzano in Italy, via the historic Brenner Pass. Repairing the wheels of old wagons and, later, the carriages of the first motor vehicles must have been a good business – at least in summer. In winter, when the pass was often closed due to snow, the young entrepreneur used his expertise with ash to fashion toboggans or sleds. Gasser Rodel (*Rodel* is German for toboggan) is now run by Christian and his brother, Thomas; their father still comes in to help out and Christian's wife does the accounts.

There are some fifteen to twenty traditional toboggan manufacturers left across the Alps; some of them comprise just one family; others are bigger than Gasser Rodel, but tobogganing has increased steadily in popularity over the last decade, largely because of the rising cost of skiing, Christian told me. He had laid out a dozen pieces of ash on the table. They included a sawn, oblong billet, a few blocks with holes or mortices cut out and something I had not seen before – two long pieces of wood bent into 'J' shapes: they were the runners of a toboggan. The wood was uniformly white. I could immediately see that the grain was straight.

'If you have grain like this,' Christian said, 'all is good. If you have grain that is very close together, that is bad. At least bad for us. We need fast-grown, healthy trees to make the best toboggans.'

Austria has nearly 40 per cent forest cover, slightly above the European average, but most of this forest is in Alpine regions. Common ash is not a major timber species, because it doesn't grow well in the mountains. In the east of the country, however, around the Danube Valley, ash grows well and is of great socio-economic and ecological import-ance. Christian buys all his ash in the states of Oberösterreich, Niederösterreich and Burgenland, along the border with Hungary where the Iron Curtain ran during the Cold War.

'My father used to choose and buy all the trees when they were standing in the forest. Sadly, we don't have time for this anymore. My brother and I visit the sawmills every year instead, and we select each tree, one by one. We do know all the forests where the trees come from and we like to see every tree in the round. We ask the sawmills to cut them to our dimensions and the timber is transported back here where it is stored outside and undercover, for one year. We never kiln-dry our timber because it dries too fast and too much, at least for steam-bending. Air-dried timber is much better for us. The quality is very, very important. We are only interested in the highest-quality timber,' Christian said, springing to his feet again and sending the chair skating across the wooden floor. Looking beyond me, out of the window and into the midday light bouncing off the mountainside across the valley, he smiled and said: 'Speaking of highest quality, where is your timber?'

When I had first contacted Christian, he had welcomed my idea of sending some ash to the Alps, to be made into a tobog-gan. However, he was very specific about both the dimensions and the grain of the two planks he required. Worried he might think my tree had grown too slowly for reincarnation as a toboggan, I picked over what was left in my barn and emailed him some photos of the best pieces. Confusion followed, partly because the photos weren't very good and partly because Christian started using German woodworking terminology, which completely stumped Google Translate. '*Riegelwuchs*', I eventually found out, means 'fiddleback' – a decorative feature sometimes found in grain: though prized by musical instrument-makers, hence the name, it can significantly reduce the strength properties of timber. Christian thought there might be fiddleback grain in my timber, rendering it useless for making toboggans.

We started going round and round in circles. I tried to tele-phone, to conclude the circumlocution of emailing. Weeks passed. In the end, I cut what I thought were the best two pieces of ash to the required dimensions, packed them into an old ski bag, booked a train ticket and left a message to say that I was coming.

'They are both good pieces of timber. I look at the grain on the end of the plank, where it's been cross-cut. Then I look down the whole length of the piece of the wood, to see how straight the grain runs. There are no failures – defects, you say in English, I think. Very often if you have even a small defect in a piece of wood and you try to steam-bend it, then it fails. Your ash is better than I expected,' Christian said, rolling up the sleeves of his plaid shirt. I silently saluted my tree. It had delivered again.

Drawing imaginary lines on my ash with his finger, Chris-tian marked out and explained where the components required to make my toboggan would come from – two runners, two support bars and two bridges. I had brought enough timber to make one and a half sleds: the extra bit was in case a piece of wood failed during the steam-bending process.

'Normally we have around 2 per cent failure rate,' Christian said. 'But we just don't know with your timber. We only bend the ash twice a week and we do it today because of your visit, but we have to go quickly now.'

The earliest record of man steam-bending wood comes from the Egyptian necropolis at Beni Hasan. Dated to the twentieth century BC, the tomb of Amenemhat, a chief priest to the pharaoh, is richly decorated with paintings depicting wrestling contests, hunting parties, the siege of a fortress and a ritual journey, as well as artisans and farmers at work. In one scene, two carpenters dressed in loincloths are shown steaming long sticks over a bowl of hot water, bending them into wide U-shapes and fixing the ends in the ground to maintain the tension while they dry.

The advantages of being able to bend wood are innumerable. While Egyptian carpenters were learning how to steam-bend ash to make bows and construct the carriages of chariots, Native Indians in North America were bending ash, and other species of wood, to create the frames of snowshoes. Elsewhere, steam-bending was used extensively in boat-building, to shape the ribs employed to reinforce hulls and make the 'knees' used as a form of bracing. The runners of sleds and skis were steam-bent in Neolithic times, so the tips didn't catch in the snow. Later, walking sticks and a multitude of tool handles fashioned for agricultural implements were heated and bent, often to make them more ergonomic. Rims for sieves and, significantly, furniture components were, and often still are, made from bent wood. The innovative *Encyclopédie ou Dictionnaire raisonné des sciences, des arts et des métiers*, compiled in France between 1751 and 1772 and one of the towering publishing achievements of the Age of Enlightenment, declared that bent ash is 'excellent to make hoops for tanks, barrels and other similar vessels'. When organized sport flourished across the modern world in the late nineteenth century, steam-bent ash was key in the manufacturing of lacrosse sticks, hockey sticks, tennis rackets, squash rackets and badminton rackets. Musical instruments, not least drums, which are often made with ash frames, include bent components today.

The cells in wood are held together and made rigid by a naturally occurring, complex, organic, glue-like substance called lignin. By applying heat and moisture to wood, it is possible to soften this lignin – a process called 'plasticization' – which allows a piece of wood to be bent. If you then fix this piece of wood in its bent form and let it cool, the lignin resets and the new shape is retained. The lignin in wood can actually be plasticized in several ways – using chemicals, in a microwave and through immersion in liquid ammonia, for example – but the use of heat and moisture in the age-old process of steam-bending remains the cheapest and most effective way.

Not all species of wood bend well. Many exotic hardwoods like utile, idigbo and African mahogany hardly bend at all. Softwoods generally bend poorly. Hardwoods from temperate regions bend best, though there is huge disparity across the species. In Europe, beech, walnut, plane, elm, maple, oak and ash bend very well, while balsa, willow and alder don't. In North America, species favoured for steam-bending include white ash, white oak, red oak, hickory and yellow birch.

In an analysis of the bending properties of different timbers, various factors have to be assessed: how far the piece of wood will bend; how likely it is to break during bending; and the potential for distortion in the bend, when the restraints are released and there is a change in the moisture content of the wood. With consideration to all these, in comparative tests to classify the bending properties of various timbers, common ash always comes out at, or very near, the top. As the ancient Egyptian carpenters came to understand, presumably through trial and error, common ash bends extraordinarily well.

'We believe ash is the best species for bending, because it stays in its bent form for ever. Some manufacturers use other types of wood, but these make cheaper toboggans. Beech is used, for example, but beech can change shape after it has been bent and cooled,' Christian said.

We were downstairs, in the bowels of the building. Thomas, Christian's brother, lifted one of my pieces of ash onto a workbench. Fixing his round, metal-rimmed glasses on his nose, he inspected it carefully. On a circular saw, he trimmed it to the correct length and then cut a triangular section out of one end. To identify the wood as mine, among the tens of thousands of pieces of ash in the factory, he wrote 'ENGLAND' on both sides. Christian explained that my stave was going into the metal steam box for two hours, at a temperature of 100 °C.

As my timber went into one steam box, plasticized ash was coming out of the other. Thomas turned the wheel that secured the door and two great jets of steam, backlit by sunlight, burst from the box, filling a corner of the room. With heavy gloves, he hauled out two identical pieces of wood roughly the same size as mine and slid them onto a battered wooden table. As the lignin in the wood does not remain plasticized for long, Thomas worked quickly, securing the wood on a thin, flexible metal tray with wedges and a lump hammer. I helped lift the tray into place on the splayed arms of the pneumatic bending machine, a great metal contraption that might have come from the torture room of a medieval dungeon. At the press of a button, the chains snapped tight and began drawing the two arms of the machine slowly up through ninety degrees into a 'U' shape, bending the two pieces of ash around a central wooden jig called a former. There was a terrific noise – a long, loud creak overlaid with a machine-gun volley of juddering, staccato cracks that rose to a frightful pitch and then slowed again to single fire before petering away. It was an extraordinary, fifteen-second auditory assault. I likened it to the sound of a wooden-hulled ship under full sail ramming into a solid shelf of sea ice.

When the machine came to rest, Thomas fixed a thick, metal bar to the two ends of the tray, which held the shape of the bent wood. The chains went slack, the arms were lowered away and the ash wood, now bent into a semi-circle at one end and secured in this shape by the metal bar, came free. The tray was hoisted onto a stack of identical trays, to be left to cool for two days while the bend set. The tray and bar compress the outer side of the bend to stop the wood from splitting, a common occurrence. Then the restraining bar and the metal tray are removed and the pieces of bent ash are stacked and left to dry for two to three weeks, depending on moisture content.

Thomas returned to the steam box. Great plumes hissed into the rafters again. As he began the bending process with the next two pieces of ash, I wandered around the factory. There were towers of bent runners, forty high and twenty deep, stacked neatly with small gaps between them, from floor to ceiling in all directions: it was like being in an ash maze. Climbing up one wall, there was a rack of eighteen, uniquely shaped runners: some were bent through a semi-circle; on others, the curve was a more languid forty-five degrees. Between them, they encompassed the range of runners for the different toboggans Gasser Rodel make, from elite racing machines to family sleds. There were box trolleys full of off-cuts, stacks of small blocks with tenons cut and ranks of laths that could have belonged in the armoury of a riot police squadron. In one corner, two laminated ash runners, used in the assembly of the most expensive sleds, were clamped to jigs while the glue set.

When Thomas had finished bending the batch of ash staves in the steam box, he led me into the woodworking shop next door, to demonstrate how the other components of a toboggan were prepared. I speak no German and Thomas spoke no English, but he had a gentle, schoolmasterly manner. Using sign language and props, he ensured that I understood what was happening and why. If he was mystified that I had travelled halfway across a continent to see wood being sawn up, he disguised it well.

Thomas set a previously steam-bent, dry piece of ash on a sophisticated CNC saw. Three minutes later, it had been milled, rounded at the ends, bored for screws, sanded and sliced down the middle to provide two runners, which were then marked with the same number. The pair would now be used in the same toboggan.

Taking the other piece of timber which I had brought, Thomas marked out, cut and shaped two rods of ash to make the supports that connect the top of the bent runners to the bridges. The offcut from this was sawn into oblong blocks on the circular saw. These were trimmed, planed, bored with angled mortice holes, glued together on a pneumatic jig and sanded, to make the two bridges of my toboggan. Thomas handled the wood several dozen times: his manual dexterity was palpable and I was not surprised to learn that he had trained as a carpenter. He also ran visual checks on the wood through every stage of the process. Not only was he looking for defects in the timber that might affect its longevity in use, he was also continually assessing how to make best use of the strength inherent in the tree, my tree. I thought if ash trees had a voice, they would commend Thomas for maximizing their potential in life after death.

Back upstairs, Christian showed me the blacksmithing workshop where strips of steel alloy were fixed to the runners. In the heart of the space, atop a wooden stump, was a great horned anvil. The workbenches next door, where the seats of the toboggans were woven, were empty. The light coming through the windows from the valley was weakening. The employees had all gone home.

At the far end of the factory, hundreds of toboggans stood ready to be shipped to shops and snow-bound homes across the Continent. There were dozens of different models, from sleek 'Supersport' racing machines that meet the Austrian Luge Federation regulations, to basic rental toboggans. There were one-seater, one-and-a-half-seater and two-seater models in child, youth and adult sizes: some of them were painted; some sleds had different track widths; their seats came in a multitude of colours and the runners came in a feast of different curves, curls, loops and arches. All the toboggans, however, had one thing in common: they were made from ash.

'We make around 10,000 toboggans a year,' Christian said. 'Every village, not just here in the Tyrol but in the Alps, has a toboggan track. In winter you walk up, maybe there is a restaurant at the top and you toboggan down. There are many races every weekend. It is popular at night too, by moonlight. As a recreation, tobogganing is increasing in popularity again. It's a big change.'

Tobogganing first became a popular recreation over a century ago, shortly before Christian's great-great-uncle set up in business – around the time my tree germinated, in fact. The inaugural 'international' toboggan race took place in Davos, Switzerland, in 1883: it was testament to the Alps emerging as a fashionable tourist destination. Holiday-makers looking for something more dynamic than taking the mineral waters and breathing the clean, mountain air were inspired by the basic transport sleds used in the age-old fashion to deliver goods through the snowbound streets of the mountain resort.

As the oldest vehicle known to man, we can only guess at the origins of the sled. It has been used to transport cargo for thousands of years. During the Mesolithic period, it was man's major work vehicle almost everywhere. When the wheel was invented, however, the development of the sled continued in geographic areas with year-round snow cover, or at least heavy annual snowfalls. The great aboriginal peoples in the circum-polar homelands of North America and Eurasia, like the Inuit and the Sami, adapted the sled to their own needs – for trav-elling on sea ice, to be pulled by dogs or reindeer and for transporting people. While these sleds were always made from wood, there is no hint of a particular species being preferen-tially used, even during the Iron Age. People simply made the best of whatever timber was available to them.

Ash first came to feature prominently in the construction of sleds and toboggans during the 'Heroic Age of Polar Exploration' in the late nineteenth and early twentieth cen-turies, when the strength-to-weight ratio of materials became a critical issue. The great explorer, scientist and later Nobel Peace Prize-winner Fridtjof Nansen, who set off to cross Greenland in 1888, took sleds made of ash with elm run-ners. His classic design, called the Nansen sled, was later copied by nearly everybody else involved in exploration on snow and ice.

Roald Amundsen learnt much about the use of sleds and

dogs for the transportation of goods from the Netsilik Inuit community on King William Island in the Canadian Arctic archipelago, during his successful expedition to traverse the Northwest Passage between the Atlantic and Pacific oceans, which departed in 1903. The sleds he later had constructed for his successful expedition to reach the South Pole in 1911 were, like Nansen's, made from Norwegian ash with runners of American hickory. Pulled by teams of dogs (some of which Amundsen's men famously ate, providing a vital source of vitamin C), these sleds made the 3,000-kilometre round trip from the Bay of Whales to the South Pole and back. As Amundsen later wrote: 'This is the greatest factor – the way in which the expedition is equipped . . . Victory awaits him who has everything in order – luck, people call it.'

The finest polar sleds are still made from steam-bent ash today. The Danish defence unit known as the Sirius Patrol has been conducting military surveillance and maintaining Denmark's sovereignty over 160,000 square kilometres of north and north-east Greenland for over sixty years, by dog sled. Each autumn, the six teams of two men who conduct the winter-long patrol build their own sleds. The runners and the structural boards of the sleds are made from clean, knot-free, straight-grained ash. The wood is tied together with nylon line, to provide extra flexibility over the rugged terrain. The sleds weigh around 80 kg and carry loads of up to 400 kg.

The properties that make ash ideal for sleds also made it useful in the construction of other items used in polar endeavour – snowshoes and skis. Rear Admiral Richard E. Byrd, the pioneering American aviator and explorer, took

snowshoes made of American white ash on many of his out-
landish expeditions in the early twentieth century. The
manufacture of snowshoes, involving the skills of the leather
worker, the weaver and the woodworker, was highly developed
among the Native Indians of North America when the first
Europeans arrived. The wood frames were soaked and heated,
then bent by hand around frames, before being cooled and
dried. Several species of wood with good bending properties
were used, including birch and larch. Wherever white ash
grew, however, it was preferred. Originally devised as a means
of walking in deep snow thousands of years ago, and probably
used by many indigenous peoples across the Polar regions,
snowshoes were adopted by the early French trappers in Canada and then by the urban masses. Walking on snowshoes
became a popular recreational pursuit in Montreal in the
mid-nineteenth century and the number of businesses manufacturing them proliferated. White ash was the main species
of wood used, until plastic and aluminium came into favour
in the middle of the twentieth century.

Skiing is another ancient form of transport devised by man
to make travel across frozen surfaces more efficient. Over
200 prehistoric skis have been uncovered, some dated to
3,000 BC. Nomadic hunters, herders and, later, farmers made
their own in a multitude of regional variations based on local
snow conditions and terrain. The skis were plain, utilitarian
instruments: they were roughly fashioned from whatever
material grew nearby – spruce, birch, willow, rowan, elm, oak
and ash were all used.

The modern ski, something that we would be able to use

today, emerged from the Telemark region of Norway in the mid-nineteenth century. Lean and graceful with a narrow waist, steam-bent, upturned tips and a symmetrically cambered middle for better control, these skis opened up the mountains to a burgeoning metropolitan population eager to learn new ways to fill their increasing leisure time. Skis were still made from a variety of different woods, but from the 1880s they were manufactured in new factories, first in Norway and then the USA. As the design was refined, so, too, was the choice of materials.

Henry Hoek, a leading ski designer during the initial boom, wrote in *How to Ski*, published in 1910: 'The choice of wood must be limited to ash and hickory.' Flexible, dense and durable, hickory quickly became the popular choice for skis in North America, where it was widely available. Several Norwegian ski-makers even moved to the USA, establishing a manufacturing centre around St Paul, Minnesota. These businesses made sleds, snowshoes and ice hockey sticks out of white ash, while the market for hickory skis grew and grew.

Hickory was first imported from the USA to Norway in 1882. Convinced that it was the best wood in extreme cold, Amundsen took hickory skis to the South Pole in 1911. It was, however, expensive: ash continued to be favoured in Europe. Genuine concern about the continuing availability of common ash in Europe, however, prompted ski-makers in Norway to develop the first laminated or composite skis in the 1890s.

The idea of artificial, laminated skis only grabbed the

attention of the world in the 1930s, by which time they were light and durable with good torsional strength. It was the end for plain skis carved from a single piece of wood, and the beginning of the end for wood altogether. Head introduced aluminium and plywood composite skis in 1947; Rossignol and Kneissl pioneered fibreglass skis in the 1950s. In the white heat of advances in manmade materials, and in successive attempts to make skis incrementally lighter and marginally easier to turn, wood was abandoned.

'My father made skis from ash, and hickory. The hickory was imported from the USA but only after the Second World War, and it was expensive. Perhaps he was one of the last manu-facturers of wooden skis. Nobody makes ash skis anymore. It's a shame, but ash is still used in Austria for furniture and particularly tool handles,' Christian told me. We were back downstairs. My ash stave had been hauled from the steam box, thrust into the jaws of the machine and bent through ninety degrees. Thomas had then carefully inspected it, for any evidence of compression failure on the inside of the bend. It was fine. The tray was placed on one side with the other components. When the runners were dry in two to three weeks, Christian would assemble my toboggan by hand. Steel runners and a seat would be attached. It would be varnished, packaged up and dispatched to Britain.

'The varnish is to look good more than anything, and so that it cleans easily. People think water is a problem with ash, but it's not true. If the toboggan gets wet for a day and then it's stored inside, you don't have a problem. If it sits outside getting wet for a year, that's a problem. I wish you a lot of snow this winter,' Christian said, laughing, as he clasped my hand. Walking back along the road to the railway station, I thought of the Black Mountains covered in snow. If I listened carefully, I could already hear my children whooping with glee.

CHAPTER 7

Clash of the Ash

'. . . ek the hardy asshe'
Geoffrey Chaucer, *The Parlement of Foules*

The day before I travelled to Ireland, I rang the Dublin City Gallery, home of the Hugh Lane collection. The painting I wanted to see – *The Tipperary Hurler* – was not currently on display. It is part of the permanent, revolving collection. Then, half an hour later, the Head of Collections emailed me. I was in luck. The portrait by Seán Keating was due to be re-hung in the Gallery on Parnell Square that night. It would be on view by the time I arrived at midday. How typical of Ireland, I thought, a country full of unsolicited gifts.

Following the creation of the Irish Free State in 1921, Keating painted a series of canvases that expressed both his empathy for the Nationalist cause and his conviction that the Irish people were capable of self-governance. *The Tipperary Hurler* is part of this series. The subject is a composite of two men who happened to look alike. Keating made the initial sketch of John-Joe Hayes, a famous Tipperary hurler, as he left the field at Croke Park, Dublin, the home of Gaelic sport, following the 1925 All-Ireland hurling final. The other subject is Ben O'Hickey, a former IRA man. By 1925, O'Hickey was an artist studying under Keating. A few years earlier, during the Uprising in Ireland, O'Hickey had been a Sinn Fein activist involved in a series of attacks and ambushes on the British government. In 1920, during the Anglo-Irish War, he was captured and sentenced to death. On the morning of his execution, the sentence was altered to penal servitude for life; on the restoration of peace, he was released.

The Tipperary Hurler was hanging in the first room beyond the reception in the Dublin City Gallery, between paintings by Paul Henry and Jack Butler Yeats. Finished in 1928, the oil painting is of a rugged, stalwart man wearing a blood-red, short-sleeved jersey, set in a beautiful landscape. The thin, ethereal light of rural Ireland leaks through clefts in the clouds. Standing in front of the canvas, I was first struck by the might of the man. His face is cocked sideways but the eyes, weighted with steel, stare down on the observer. The high cheekbones, the heavy eyebrows, the pursed lips, the six o'clock shadow and the ribs of strained sinew in his neck create an impression of vigour and independence. Clasped in the man's heavy hands, ready to be driven into the land or raised to smite an adversary, is a smooth, white stave crafted into an oblique shape. Few outside Ireland would know what this stave is. For the Irish, however, it is a national emblem, a totem as ubiquitous as Guinness: a hurley stick made from ash.

Hurling is one of Ireland's ancient, native games. The objective of the players on two teams is to hit a small ball or *sliotar* between the opponents' goalposts with a wooden stick called a hurley or 'hurl' – in the Irish language, a *camán*.

The ball can be caught and carried, struck in mid-air or hit on the ground with the hurley. There are plenty of other rules, but really, to get the gist of it, you need to watch a game. It is thought to be the world's fastest and most skilful game. It is also likely to be the oldest extant field sport known to man.

The origins of hurling predate our recorded history. The Book of Leinster, an epic of early Irish heroic literature, includes an account of the battle of Moytura, supposedly fought in County Mayo in 1272 BC, between the native Fir Bolg and the Tuatha de Danann. While the two tribes were preparing for battle, some of the men engaged in a hurling contest, which was played until 'their bones were broken and bruised and they fell outstretched on turf'.

The Book of Leinster also documents the feats of Setanta, better known as Cú Chulainn, the most significant figure in Celtic mythology and a sort of Irish Achilles. Raised in a remote part of Ulster, Cú Chulainn learnt to hurl 'above a mortal pitch'. While travelling, he would strike the ball a long distance into the air, fling his hurley after it and race forward like the wind to catch them both. Of course, the Book of Leinster is not an historical record, though many of the tales of Cú Chulainn do entwine aspects of historical fact and occasionally correspond with archaeological findings. It is a compilation of oral, vernacular tales that probably date from the centuries before the birth of Christ, and in its pages hurling becomes a metaphor for strength and dexterity.

Hurling first emerges into the light of history through the ancient Irish civil code known as Brehon law: the field game is mentioned as a means to settle disputes between towns or villages as early as the eighth century. The famous Statutes of Kilkenny, passed in 1366 in an attempt to arrest the steady amalgamation of the Anglo-Norman barons into Gaelic life, forbade the barons and their retinues from 'games which men call hurlings, with great clubs, of a ball, on the ground from which great evils have arisen'. The Statute of Galway of 1537 outlawed the playing of hurling altogether.

It is fair to assume people ignored the ban and continued to play hurling because by the middle of the seventeenth century there were numerous clergymen condemning it. By the eighteenth century, the gentry and other large landowners fielded teams of their tenants and inter-barony, or inter-province, hurling matches were born. There was still no standard size for pitches or goals, teams varied in numbers and there were no referees. Rules were simply agreed before each match, but these games were great social affairs with crowds, hospitality tents and gambling. Matches were even recorded in the national newspapers.

What has been called the 'golden age' of hurling, and the patronage that provided for it, died out, though. The unsuccessful Irish Rebellion of 1798, the Act of Union that followed, the Napoleonic Wars, the disruption of rural society caused by the famines of the mid-nineteenth century and the suppression of Irish culture by the British authorities were all factors. By the 1880s, the brilliant, dynamic athletic game that had provided a remarkable continuity in Irish sporting and cultural life over millennia had almost been wiped out.

On a dank evening in November 1884, in the billiard room of Hayes Hotel in Thurles, County Tipperary, the Gaelic Athletic Association (GAA) was founded. The initial aim was the preservation and cultivation of Irish athletics, but the GAA was almost immediately caught in the revival of political and cultural awareness that was sweeping Ireland at the time. Hurling, along with the other historic and uniquely Irish field sport, Gaelic football, was soon being codified by the GAA and promoted as a form of nationalistic self-expression. Quickly, hurling took its place as the passionate articulation of a people's soul, at a time when the British were still curbing so much other native culture, most notably the Irish language. The game still holds that place today. Arguably, the GAA rescued the ancient game of hurling, or at least a version of it, from the grave.

By the time Ben O'Hickey was in prison and John-Joe Hayes was emerging as a star hurler, however, the game had moved on again, to become a conciliatory and unifying influence on a country divided first by an Anglo-Irish War (1919–21), and then a Civil War (1922–3).

The early success of the GAA in reviving hurling was partly due to the Parish Rule, whereby every parish had its own GAA club. During the 1930s, nationalism began to dissolve and local identity proudly renewed itself again. As with rugby union in the coal-mining valleys of South Wales, territorial loyalty became a force bonding GAA clubs from within.

There were plenty of disputes between clubs over the interpretation of new rules adopted by the GAA, but the differences were ironed out as the importance of the national championship, inaugurated in 1887, grew and grew. Today, the All-Ireland Senior Hurling Championship is a social phenomenon: it is a great gathering of the clans which defines autumn for a large part of the Irish population. It was the reason I had come to Dublin.

Outside the Dublin City Gallery, I fell into a stream of red and blue running down the road towards Croke Park. I had a ticket to see the All-Ireland semi-final match between Dublin and Cork – my first ever hurling match. The city centre was rinsed in sunshine and rippling with anticipation, not least because Dublin last won the All-Ireland Hurling Championship seventy-five years ago. The legions of fervent Dublin fans believed 2013 was going to be their year.

Hurling long ago fulfilled its role in the rediscovery of Irish identity; but it is no longer a political game. It has evolved to become a cherished part of the national character; it is a unifying and identifying thread through Irish life, like the grain through the ash sticks they use to play it. I had noticed, on many previous visits to Ireland, that you see hurley sticks everywhere: on the shoulder of a man walking home from the GAA club in the dying light of a summer's day; on the seat of a car outside the supermarket; leaning against a pub wall; and in the hands of a boy, banging a *sliotar* against the gable end of his house after school, in the rain.

There is, perhaps, a lingering sense of snobbery attached

to the game: enthusiasm for and knowledge of hurling can still be a measure of Celtic purity. More importantly, though, hurling remains an amateur game: the players that perform wonders on the pitch in front of tens of thousands one day might be servicing your boiler or fixing the clutch on your car the next. This fundamental aspect soaks through every level of the sport, from the humble demeanour of the greatest players through the appreciation of the fans, to the manner of the turnstile attendants at Croke Park on big match days.

You will not hear many English accents at an All-Ireland Hurling semi-final, yet almost every time I opened my mouth, someone wanted to help. Queuing to buy a pint in a bar on Gardiner Place, I got the run-down on how the teams had reached the semi-final: the season was already being dubbed the best hurling championship in thirty years.

Inside the ground, a security manager let me slip through a locked gate so I could visit the GAA Museum before the match. When I finally got onto the terraces, a minute before the game started, it was crammed to the hilt, but I caught a man's eye and he enthused his mates to edge inches along the concrete and let me in. I had bought a ticket to stand on Hill 16, home of the Dublin fans and the guts of Croke Park, following the advice of a lady in the GAA press office: 'It's where the craic is, all right,' she'd said. 'You'll be grand there, so long as you don't mind a little blaspheming.'

The game was electric from the off. Dublin scored after twelve seconds. A minute later, Cork scored. Two minutes after that, Cork scored again. The *sliotar* flew from one end of the green field to the other in a fury of perpetual motion.

The white hurley sticks swirled and gleamed as they caught the sunlight. From the terraces they looked like wands. To be made into a hurley stick and used in the All-Ireland Senior Hurling Championship at Croke Park was, I reflected, a noble end for an unexceptional piece of ash.

The catching, the blocking, the running, the side-stepping, the scooping of the *sliotar* off the grass by players in full flight, the deft passing and the striking of the ball out of hand were remarkable. I could hardly keep up.

'Clash of the ash. Fookin' great,' exclaimed Mickey, who'd made space for me on the terraces, shunting an elbow into my ribs. He leaned back and bellowed at the sky: 'C'mon the Dubs!'

Mickey had generously offered to explain anything I didn't understand but we soon realized this wouldn't work: things were happening too fast on the pitch. Twice he turned to talk into my ear – when a Dublin player got a yellow card and then when the *sliotar* went into touch – and both times Cork scored. 'Bollix,' he said, 'We'll speak at half-time.'

After twenty-five minutes, the score had been levelled seven times. After half an hour, Dublin scored a goal, worth three points, and Hill 16 went wild. When the whistle went for half-time, the crowd of 62,000 exhaled as one. Everyone, it seemed, had been holding their breath. I wondered if I had ever seen a more exhilarating thirty-five minutes of sport. The ball can travel almost the length of the field in one mighty swat with a hurley stick, at speeds of up to 90 mph, giving a distinct and dynamic choreography to the game. There is a balletic quality to running with the ball, tipping it on the hurley stick, and to the twists and whirls players perform to get a clean strike. This grace and dexterity is married to moments of medieval thuggery, when the players make contact with each other. Someone had described hurling to me as a cross between hockey and homicide: I thought it was more like ballet on crack cocaine.

The defining moment in the match came fifteen minutes into the second half. The Dublin centre forward was sent off, tipping an immaculately balanced game in favour of Cork, the 'Rebel County'. With ten minutes to go, the game was gone. It would have been Dublin's first All-Ireland Hurling final for fifty-two years. Mickey didn't speak again.

It had been tumultuous: forty-five scores in seventy minutes; the teams had been level on fifteen occasions. I had arrived at Croke Park as a neutral, but I'd been swept away by the urgency of the Dublin fans and I was disappointed. Walking away from Croke Park, I remembered a description of hurling that I'd read: 'a game invented by the gods and played by men'. At least I now understood what this meant.

The next day, I set off from Dublin to County Waterford to visit a hurley stick maker. Halfway, I made a detour to a small village in the shadow of the mountain, Slievenamon, in the south-east corner of County Tipperary, to meet Liam and Danny Murray of Woodelo. These enterprising young brothers were developing a new use for ash. At least, they were reviving a long-forgotten use for ash – they were making bicycle frames. As a lifelong cyclist and the owner of eleven bicycles, I had to test-ride an ash frame.

'My family background is in farming and I've always been interested in wood,' Liam told me. 'Growing up around here, we rode mountain bikes in the forestry all the time. There wasn't a lot of local entertainment back then. If you weren't playing hurling, you rode your bike.'

We were walking around the Woodelo workshop. I've spent plenty of time with bespoke bike-builders: the tools, machines and various workstations were all familiar, but I had never put my hands on a modern bicycle frame made from wood before. The earliest ancestors of the bicycle, the Draisine in the early nineteenth century, and later the 'hobby horse', were made from wood – often ash – as were the wheels, and I had seen these machines in museums but I had never before sat on a wooden frame.

'We knew from hurley sticks that ash is a strong material,' Liam said. 'It seemed an obvious choice, so we had a go. We made the first frame from ash and it worked. It was dog-heavy and it's taken us three years to develop it to this stage. The road bike frames now weigh about 2 kg, though weight is not the priority. Making the frames functional and aesthetically pleasing is the focus.'

We stopped beside a bike mounted in a workstand. It looked like a road-racing bicycle should – good geometry, drop handlebars, arrowhead saddle and lightweight wheels – but the frame was clearly ash. I marvelled at it. 'It's lovely timber to work,' Liam said, taking the bike out of the stand and wheeling it towards me. 'It's not prone to splitting. It's very tactile. We can machine it and strengthen it where we want. Its usability is astonishing. But really, we love it because of its shock-absorbing characteristics. It's very, very comfortable. It's better than a carbon frame in my opinion. Fancy a ride?'

We pedalled for a couple of hours along lanes through the green land between Slievenamon and the Slieveardagh hills. It was a lovely ride. The bicycle felt comfortable, though I'm sure my appreciation of the mechanical properties of the ash was affected by my sheer delight at riding through the countryside on a sustainable resource, something nature created. Inevitably, we passed dozens, perhaps hundreds of ash trees in the hedgerows: the ash is an important, native tree species in Ireland – economically, environmentally and culturally.

In Irish mythology, the ash belongs to the trilogy of sacred trees and was associated with healing, protection and divination. Druids' wands were often made of ash. The mythic 'Branching Tree of Uisneach', which is supposed to have stood on the Hill of Uisneach at the centre point of Ireland, was an ash. In legend, it was planted by Fintan the Ancient. According to Robert Graves in *The White Goddess*, it fell in AD 665, symbolizing the triumph of Christianity, preached by St Patrick, over paganism.

Graves also records that a descendant of the Sacred Tree of Creevna, again an ash, stood outside a churchyard in County Cork in the early nineteenth century. The wood from this venerated tree was thought to be a charm against drowning (as ash often was in folklore). Following the potato famine, emigrants to America whittled chips off the tree before setting sail, until there was nothing left of it.

Back in the Woodelo workshop, Liam almost had to prise

me off the bicycle. As a connoisseur of two wheels, I desperately wanted one. At around £2,000 a frame, though, I would have to wait.

'Carving the stays, sanding the tubes down until they're perfect and hand-finishing the frames – it's very time-consuming work,' Liam said. 'People have forgotten about the versatility of ash. They think it's just good for firewood, even in Ireland, where we are familiar with the ash through hurley sticks. It's hard trying to change people's perceptions, but we're going to try.'

'You saw the game of the year,' Frank Murphy said. 'You have the good luck, then. So that's it.' Frank, in his mid-fifties, was tall and thin with broad, rolled shoulders. There was a hint of former athletic prowess in his long, steady gait. With a clean-shaven jaw, whiskers along his cheekbones and eyes that smiled brilliantly as he listened, he could have been the kindly woodcutter from a fairytale.

We were walking through woodland on the Curraghmore Estate owned by Lord Waterford, near the village of Portlaw in County Waterford. The summer had been hot and dry. The woodland floor rustled and crackled under the weight of our boots. Behind us, the Clodiagh river was whispering its way from the Comeragh Mountains to meet the mighty river Suir. We walked slowly, pausing in the glades where the sun fell in heated hoops. I felt the sense of antiquity that is common enough in woodlands. The ash trees – tall, slender and smooth-barked – grew randomly between eminent oaks, the odd birch and hazel stools cloaked in ivy.

Frank stopped, dug his hands deep into his pockets and looked up into the canopy: ''Tis a beautiful place. I'd say that a man would live for ever here.'

Frank Murphy is a hurley stick-maker, as his uncle and his great-uncle were before him. He has been converting ash timber into the magical wands I'd seen whirling around Croke Park the day before, for thirty-five years. When we first spoke, I had garbled my plan down the telephone – to bring a piece of my ash tree from Wales to Ireland, for him to craft into a hurley stick. When I described my tree, though – 125 years old, circumference of 190 centimetres at chest height, a bole 5.5 metres in length – he had gently deflated my enthusiasm.

Though ash grows readily throughout much of Ireland, the right conditions for quality hurley ash are very precise. Trees must be grown on good, level ground with free draining soil, ideally with a pH of six or seven. Standing water impairs root formation while ash grown on gravelly soil can be brittle. Most importantly, ash trees used in the manufacture of hurley sticks are felled at twenty-five to forty years old, depending on growth rate and quality. Only the bottom part of the tree, from ground level to a height of 1.3 metres, is utilized: the point where the base of the tree flares out into the roots provides the natural shape of the stick. These root buttresses, the strongest bit of the tree, form the part of the hurley stick used to strike the *sliotar*, known as the 'boss' or '*bás*'. The rest of the tree, above the height of 1.3 metres, is then used in a variety of other ways, including the manufacture of tool handles, furniture production and firewood.

'You can only make a good hurley stick from good hurley ash. That's why it is so expensive,' Frank had said on the phone. 'Come over to Waterford and I'll show you some fine hurley ash trees. I'll even make you a stick, but I can't do it with your ash. So that's it.'

We had walked a mile through the wood but we hadn't found a fine hurley ash tree yet. Frank had dismissed many of the trees as too young and too old. Several had inadequate root formation. One tree had evidence of knots low down on the trunk. Another he disregarded at a glance – 'a bit of rot and likely a black line down the middle. No good.' Sometimes he simply didn't like the bark. I had read that the characteristics of the wood can sometimes be inferred from the appearance of the bark: if the furrows of bark spiral up a tree, it is likely the wood does too; where the bark has healed over dead branches, knots lie underneath; soft bark with long flakes is an indicator of slow-growth and tight-grained wood. Watching Frank, I thought of Giles Winterborne in Thomas Hardy's *The Woodlanders*. Winterborne knew the 'tongue of the trees': he could tell with one look if a trunk had a sound heart or incipient rot.

'Now, this looks a good one,' Frank said, stepping briskly off the path. He crouched beside the base of a slim, straight tree about 45 centimetres in diameter. With his hand, he roughed the grass and ivy covering the roots and then dug hard at the soil with the heel of his boot. 'You could have a quality hurley out of here,' he said, running his hand down the trunk and over the bulbous toes where they met the earth. 'That's a very nice root, and again in the back there, and a little one here. You'd have a good few sticks out of that. You cut the butt into planks for hurleys. You might get six out of that toe, three there and maybe three here. So you might get a dozen hurleys out of this tree.

'If Lord Waterford was cutting out a wood, well now, he'd give me a ring. We'd go round the wood together and mark the good trees with an axe. I'd aim to cut maybe sixty or more trees and we'd negotiate a price, then I'd be round again to take out the ash myself, before any other felling would be done.'

I had read that 450,000 hurleys are manufactured and sold each year. For the last fifteen years, there has been a shortage of high-quality, home-grown ash, partly because hurling, and the women's game called camogie, are growing in popularity. Frank still manages to procure all his butts within Ireland, because he keeps in touch with the people who are growing ash trees well. Many hurley-makers, however, have to import their ash butts from the UK and the Continent. I know of several woodland owners near me in Wales and Herefordshire who sell ash to hurley stick-makers.

The agriculture and food development department of the Irish government, Teagasc, has invested time and scientific endeavour in a large-scale effort to improve the quality and volume of hurley ash for the future, by propagating the best trees and enhancing growing methods. There were hopes that a major afforestation scheme would make Ireland self-sufficient in ash in the near future. Sadly, ash dieback disease will inevitably impact on those hopes.

*

Wandering back to Frank's truck, I asked about alternative materials to ash. Rowan and cherry have been tried, he told me. Willow makes a very light hurley and it lasts well, but you seldom find a tree wide enough to make the boss. Frank thought that every species of tree that grows in Ireland would have been tried at some point, but ash has been prized as the best for as long as reliable records exist.

Initially, ash would have been favoured through trial and error: ash hurley sticks simply broke less often than sticks made out of other woods. We now know that the mechanical properties of ash, particularly toughness and elasticity, make it an ideal material for smashing a *sliotar* up and down the green fields of Ireland. There is one other mechanical property of ash that makes it excellent for hurley sticks – it has great bending strength, often referred to as modulus of rupture, or MOR for short.

MOR is a measure of the maximum load-carrying capacity of a piece of wood loaded perpendicular to its long axis, and it is a widely accepted criterion of strength in determining safe working stresses in structural timbers for engineering. As with modulus of elasticity, values for MOR are only indicative and they vary within tree species according to many factors. The MOR value becomes useful, however, in comparison with other species of wood. The figure often given for air-dried (12 per cent moisture content), defect-free ash is higher than all other European hardwoods, with the exception of beech and hornbeam, though it should be noted that the dataset is small. Oak, often the benchmark in considering the strength properties of wood, has an MOR value some 20 per cent lower than ash.

The dominance of ash in the manufacture of hurley sticks quite possibly set the precedent for its wider use in other sports. For much of the history of modern field hockey, the sticks were made from ash. Cricket stumps and bails were traditionally made from ash: the best ones still are. Shinty, a field game similar to hockey and native to the west coast of Scotland, was traditionally played with sticks made from ash. Parallel bars and other pieces of gymnasium apparatus are made out of ash, as are the handles of polo sticks and croquet mallets.

The asymmetric frames of real tennis rackets have been made in Paris from ash since the late Middle Ages. Celebrated craftsmen boiled and bent selected staves of ash before clamping them to a mould, to form the distinctive lopsided racket heads. The frames were then pierced, sanded, oiled, polished and sometimes smoked over burning sawdust.

Racquets rackets were made from ash. Henry John Gray, the leading racquets player of his day, founded Grays of Cambridge in 1855. For over a century, Grays made the finest rackets and hockey sticks from English ash. My big brother had a Grays squash racket in pale, varnished ash when we were kids. For several decades through the middle of the twentieth century, the Dunlop corporation bought tens of thousands of cubic feet of ash annually, from the best ash-growing counties in the UK – Herefordshire, Shropshire, Sussex and parts of Kent – as well as from Normandy and the Belgian Ardennes. During this period, ash even became known as 'the sportsman's wood'.

The huge volume of high-grade ash purchased by Dunlop

went into the production of squash, badminton and tennis rackets. The Dunlop Maxply racket, first sold in 1931, became the most popular tennis racket in the world. As a child, I owned a Dunlop Maxply; by the 1970s, they were made from several species of laminated wood, including ash. On my twelfth birthday in 1979, I upgraded to a Wilson Vitus Gerulaitis Pro, also made of laminated ash. I've still got it, which says more about my capacity to hoard than it does about the value of the racket.

Wilson also made the first aluminium tennis racket in 1967, though metal only began to seriously challenge the pre-eminence of wood when Jimmy Connors won Wimbledon with a Wilson T2000 tubular-steel racket in 1974. That wasn't the end of wood, though: the last 'wooden racket' Wimbledon final, between Bjorn Borg and John McEnroe, took place in 1980. It is regarded by aficionados as the greatest final ever played.

Around this time, manufacturers began to experiment with composite frames, made possible by the development of carbon fibre. By the early 1980s, the ash tennis racket was heading for the museum. In 1982, more non-wood rackets were sold than wood ones. For many, the game has slowly deteriorated ever since: adherents of wooden rackets believe that touch, finesse, control, nuance and strategy have been replaced by power, largely because of the modern materials used in the construction of rackets.

During the 1970s, some hurley stick manufacturers experimented with plastic, but it led to an increase in player injuries. Fifteen years ago, the carbon fibre hurley was introduced.

People said it was going to take over, but it splintered too easily and the authorities withdrew it from the market. There have been umpteen attempts to replace ash, yet the technologies behind the array of increasingly sophisticated materials have so far been unable to equal its properties, including weight, appearance, price, performance, game-handling, elasticity and strength. It is extraordinary that, in the twenty-first century, a skilfully made hurley stick from well-grown ash will rule over any other material every time.

One wall of Frank's workshop was covered in photos of famous hurling matches and star players. Many, including Christy Ring, a Cork maestro from the middle of the twentieth century, stood with sticks cocked high above their heads, ready to strike the *sliotar* into the neighbouring county. Pride of place went to photos of the All-Ireland Waterford teams of 1948 and 1959. Along another wall, a hundred or so new hurley sticks were racked up, awaiting buyers, and their moment of glory. A cabinet behind the makeshift sales counter housed a collection of old hurley sticks. Frank pulled one out to show me: it was a replica of the stick used by a Kilkenny great, Lory Meagher, in the 1920s, and different to the sticks used today.

'The game has changed and the shape of the hurley has changed with it. In the old days, players struck the ball on the ground more and the stick had a bigger sweep on the boss,' Frank said. 'Now the game is all picking and running. The hurleys are shorter and a little lighter, around 1 lb 4 or 5 ounces. The boss is getting wider and the nose is shaped. Modern pitches are like golf courses, the grass is so short. The nose of the boss has to be sharper, so you can hop the ball up. The shape is evolving all the time. So that's it.'

The process of making the sticks has changed too, Frank explained. Modern machine tools have taken the place of saws, hatchets, spokeshaves and hand planes: 'It was hard work back then, but ash is beautiful wood to work with that way, and you'd learn so much from it as well. We'd finish a stick with a bit of broken glass. It was like peeling an orange and you'd get a grand finish. It took longer, but they weren't calling time money back then,' he said.

While he was preparing the workshop, Frank explained the process to me: the butt of the ash tree travels from the wood to the sawmill, where it is quartered and sawn into planks 1 inch thick. These are then dried. Hurley stick-makers want ash dried to around 15 per cent moisture content. A lot of ash for the hurley market is dried in kilns nowadays, though Frank prefers the old way: he leaves the boards stacked up and criss-crossed in his workshop to air-dry for six to nine months.

When a sense of order had been restored in the workshop, Frank rubbed his hands together and glanced around the room. We were ready. He lifted a board off the stack of timber that had come from a wood in County Tyrone. He held the board upright for me to inspect, by the open door where the sunlight was angling in. 'To me now, that's beautiful,' he said, running a finger along the lines of annual rings in the wood, from the top of the board to the toe. 'The run of the grain is so important. It gives the hurley the strength and the spring. And if you find a board with a knot in it, well, that's firewood.

This is a lovely piece of ash, it is. We'll make a hurley out of this one.'

With the board on a workbench, he traced the outline of a hurley in pencil using his own standard, model stick, in a Waterford shape. The board was then carefully sawn. Standing on Hill 16 at Croke Park, Mickey had told me that nearly every county has a slightly different standard shape for a hurley, to which players are very loyal. A Cork player wouldn't use a Kilkenny stick; an Antrim player wouldn't use a Clare stick, and so on. I couldn't yet tell the difference between a Waterford stick and a Tipperary stick, but I knew it would be like regional Irish brogues – when your ear eventually tunes into the diverse accents, identifying them becomes a simple, everyday pleasure.

When Frank started crafting hurleys, there were commonly one or two makers in every parish, each with their own style and secrets, passed down by word of mouth. Today, there are some sixty hurley-makers left in Ireland. Hurling has managed to resist the steady homogenization of sport in the twentieth century, partly because of craftsmen like Frank: the sticks are all handmade and every one is a little bit different.

'The weight and size of the *sliotar* is regulated, but not the hurley. So different-size players will want a different-size hurley. And anyone hurling well will also have his own idea of what he wants in a stick. See all those hurleys up there' – he pointed to several dozen old sticks on the wall – 'they're all customers' models, and every one is slightly different. Good players will have four or five identical sticks and I'd say most of them could find their own hurley in the dark. You'd have a feel for your stick, the balance, the weight, the size of the handle, and the shape of the boss. You'd know the moment you picked it up that it's right, and yours. It's like your own arm.'

Frank dabbed, pawed and stroked the ash with the electric hand-sander. Flinders leapt like embers from a hot fire and gathered in piles at the back of the bench. He worked quickly and precisely, with rhythm and considered energy. Nothing was rushed. The stick was almost continually moving in one hand and he was constantly assessing the progress of his work. Every few seconds Frank raised the stick, to eye it carefully.

Hurley sticks break when they are struck against other sticks, not when they hit the ball, Frank explained, hence the sport's nickname – 'the clash of the ash'. They can be repaired, though, by a process called 'splicing', and some players bring their favourite stick back again and again.

The sound of the belt-sanding machine starting up reverberated off the walls. When Frank pressed the ash against the sandpaper, it hissed angrily. He rolled the handle over and over, shaping it to the simian grip of the human hand. On the next, lighter belt-sander, he raised the stick more frequently, rolling it in his hands. Finally, he was satisfied. He wrapped a band of black tape 2 inches thick around the neck of the boss and applied his stamp – 'Frank Murphy, Hurley Maker, Kilmagemogue, Kilmeaden, Co. Waterford.'

Balancing the hurley on open palms, Frank held it up towards me: 'It will lighten a little as it dries out. It will shrink a tiny bit too, perhaps. Some players used to put linseed oil on their sticks, which helps keep them more pliable, but nobody bothers anymore. You do what you like, though, Rob. I made this hurley for you.'

I took the stick. It wasn't the first time I had held a hurley but it was the first time I had held my own hurley, and it was different. I'd read that the old hurley-makers used to say you gave birth to a hurley; that there is a soul in ash, which the stick-maker merely releases. It certainly felt like there was life and purpose in my stick. It was elegant to look at and delightful to hold, an object of commonplace beauty made out of unadulterated wood. I thought of the mythical hero Cú Chulainn flinging his hurley into the air, and of the Tipperary Hurler proudly clasping his own ash stave.

The stick was light but weighted in the right areas. Running my fingers over the boss, I could feel the annual growth rings of the tree. Moving my hands up and down the handle, I found them instinctively anchored in several different places. The hurley rested as easily in one hand as it did in two. I cannot play the game of hurling, but just holding the stick I felt an eagerness to learn.

As I was thanking Frank, there was a kerfuffle outside the front door of the workshop and three boys burst in, followed by their father. When the exclamations of the boys were exhausted, the father said they were five, seven and nine years old. They had come to buy their first new hurley sticks. Junior hurleys come in several sizes and Frank measured them up – the top of the hurley should reach the player's hip when the heel is on the ground – while their father urged them to pay attention. I couldn't work out who was enjoying the moment most – the boys, their father or me. Once the boys all had a hurley, there was no controlling them. They were swishing them around, clattering an old wooden chair and then the doorframe as they bounced outside where a game of fantasy hurling was unleashed.

The eldest boy pretended to flick an imaginary *sliotar* off the grass, bounce it on the boss of his stick and then, in full flight, strike it with a thunderous swipe over his shoulder for a score, no doubt in the dying moments of an All-Ireland final in front of a full house at Croke Park. Another boy was pretending to drive free hits up-field. The enthusiasm was arresting. I saw the father pay Frank and I wondered if you could put a price on your son getting his first hurley stick, a stave of native ash soused with the history and the hopes of a nation. A moment later, the boys were bundled back into the car. They drove off, clutching their new implements of magic.

CHAPTER 8

Crack of the Bat

'Every farm woodland, in addition to yielding
lumber, fuel and posts, should provide its owner a
liberal education. This crop of wisdom never fails,
but it is not always harvested.'
Aldo Leopold, *A Sand County Almanac*

Not all ash trees are created equal. Only the healthiest, most erect white ash trees with clean, straight, consistent grain are fit to be converted into the magical clubs swung with venom by professional baseball players. Hillerich & Bradsby, America's oldest and largest manufacturer of baseball bats and owner of the immortal 'Louisville Slugger' brand, source most of their ash timber from a 200-mile strip along the border between northern Pennsylvania and New York State. In fact, almost every baseball bat-maker in the country acquires ash timber from the rich, thickly carpeted deciduous forests in this corner of the USA. Factors including elevation, rainfall, warm summers, cold winters and the deep loam with gravelly subsoil combine to produce ideal growing conditions for white ash trees.

White ash (*Fraxinus Americana*) is the most important of the sixteen species of ash native to North America. Its natural range extends from Nova Scotia in Canada, west to

Wisconsin, and south as far as Texas. Like its close cousin, common ash, white ash has compound, pinnate leaves and single-winged fruit 'keys'. The timber from white ash is versatile, tough, flexible and straight-grained. In fact, the physical, mechanical and working properties, as well as the look and feel of white ash timber, are so similar to common ash that you need some expertise to distinguish them. When the first waves of emigrants arrived in the New World in the seventeenth century, they must have been reassured to find a species of tree similar to that which had been so important to domestic life in Europe for so long. The early pioneers and homesteaders soon shaped white ash into all manner of functional wares like furniture, oars, lobster traps, wheel felloes, tool handles and, eventually, the item most popularly associated with ash throughout the twentieth century, the baseball bat.

'I absolutely feel a sense of satisfaction and pride in being part of the creation of the baseball bat. It's an American icon. I'm not even a huge baseball fan, but I recognize how important the bat is culturally. I'd say there'd be a baseball bat somewhere in most American homes,' Brian Boltz, a tall, bear-like man in jeans and a plaid shirt, said. Brian is responsible for the timber division of Hillerich & Bradsby. On a perfect autumn day, I had driven through mile after mile of mountainous terrain covered in forests exploding with autumn colours to meet him at one of the three company sawmills, near the town of Warren, Pennsylvania. In this part of the country, the skills and tradition in woodworking and forestry have been maintained over generations. As the lady in the wooden village store, where I had stopped to buy a sandwich, said: 'Yup, people round here grow up with sawdust in their hair.'

The best white ash trees for baseball bats tend to grow along ridges, or on northerly and easterly exposed slopes, where the rich soil and good moisture retention result in moderately fast yearly growth. Because these environments are favourable to several hardwood species, the forests are dense with trees, forcing the ash to grow straight up towards the light, which produces clean trunks and good-quality timber.

'We take the highest-quality ash only. The rest will go to other sawmills, many of which are owned by tool handle manufacturers. Handles for rakes, hoes, shovels and axes are still made from ash here, as they always have been. Some timber will go into furniture. There's still quite a strong tradition in this part of the country of people working the ash,' Brian said.

The other two company sawmills are 100 miles and 150 miles due east of Warren, on roughly the same line of longitude and surrounded by similar mountainous terrain, cloaked in forest. Brian buys good-quality logs from anywhere in the region but most of the ash processed at this mill comes from within a 50-mile radius. Go south and the ash gets a little browner and softer, Brian explained; go north and it is whiter; go east and the trees tend to have more side branches. Head into New England and the timber gets denser and less flexible. About 40,000 trees are felled annually for Hillerich & Bradsby, to meet the needs of the wooden baseball bat market. White ash doesn't take well to planting but, like common ash, it regenerates naturally. In a forest where the timber and the deer are carefully managed, white ash will happily regrow, often at a faster rate than it is harvested, and mature into stately trees for the future.

Hillerich & Bradsby have made over 100 million baseball bats in the last century and a quarter. I had expected a huge industrial sawmill with cathedral buildings connected by raised concrete walkways, teams of trucks arriving and departing, chimneys disgorging towers of smoke, cranes, dozens of workers and stacks of timber piled to the sky in every direction, all enveloped in the piercing cacophony of whirring saws. In fact, the operation was a modest, slightly homespun set-up. It could have been a sawmill from a Richard Scarry children's book. There were no trucks or cranes. The three single-storey buildings with tinplate roofs were set irregularly on a gentle rise beside a lane. The view from almost anywhere was glorious – across fields, down into a valley and beyond, to a far hillside mantled in a carpet of autumn colours, like the dying flare of a silent explosion, illuminated against a clear blue sky.

I could make out the reds and oranges of sugar maple, the golden brown of white oak and the scarlet of red maple or dogwood. There, too, was the fading purple, the last breath of exuberance before the white ash trees adopted their austere, elegant, winter cloak. In summer, when leaf cells are full of chlorophyll (the green pigment that absorbs sunlight to provide energy for the alchemic process, photosynthesis), they absorb the blue and red light of the sun, but reflect the green intensely. In the autumn, though, when the trees 'call time' and begin to make arrangements for winter, the sap, which carries water from the soil to the leaves, stops flowing in the deciduous forest, the chlorophyll vanishes and one of the most dramatic events of plant life on earth begins.

The task of driving through New York State and Pennsylvania had been made serene by patchwork quilts of blue, orange, yellow, red, russet, tan, tawny, fawn, copper, auburn, scarlet and gold, all illuminated by the soft, autumnal sun. I had not timed my visit to the USA to coincide with this great display of tree colour – it was a happy consequence of visiting the USA to look at the production of ash baseball bats during the game's annual fanfare, the World Series, held in the last week of October.

We were standing at the entrance to the main sawmill. Logs or 'bolts' cut to 40-inch lengths were being mounted on a bespoke machine that sends a tube saw straight through the centre of the log to produce perfect, solid, 3-inch-diameter cylinders of ash called 'billets'.

'After the billets have been sawn from the log, the leftover bits of wood are sold on,' Brian explained, pointing to a crate of offcuts. 'In fact, we sell all the by-products of bat production here. The sawdust is collected too, and turned into pellets for wood-burning stoves. They buy it all. That's ash for you.'

In the neighbouring building, billets were being stacked into one of the five large kilns, which take about 12,000 billets each. They dry on a thirty-day cycle, in a process designed to mimic air-drying in summer. This, Brian explained, makes the best baseball bats in terms of strength. Kiln-drying was introduced in the 1960s: it is the biggest change in production over the last half century. Before that, the billets were air-dried for nine months to a year in a huge yard at the factory site in Louisville. There would have been a million billets drying at any time.

When the pallets of cylindrical tubes come out of the kiln, each billet is inspected again for defects, sorted by weight and grade for quality – a very important part of the whole production process – before being packed onto one of two trucks that make the journey each week to Kentucky. The billets are graded again at the factory in Louisville. There, the final decision is made on whether a billet meets the exacting requirements to be made into a professional baseball bat, a Minor League bat or a lower-quality bat for the retail market.

As we passed a trolley of billets, Brian picked one out and handed it to me. The attributes that make the timber fit for professional baseball bats were apparent, he explained: the consistent, creamy-blond colour, the absence of knots and blemishes and, critically, the straight grain running uniformly through the stick.

Though ash has been used in bat-making since the birth of baseball, manufacturers have continuously experimented with alternative tree species. At the beginning of the twentieth century, hickory was used. Renowned for its strength, and a popular choice in the manufacture of tool handles, hickory is heavier than ash, making it harder to swing smoothly. A century ago, the game was different, though. Hitters 'bunted' the ball to get to bases. Bat control was key and players were less concerned about weight. That changed with Babe Ruth, arguably the nation's first sporting hero and one of the most famous Americans of all time.

A short, powerful, rotund man, nicknamed 'the Sultan of Swat', Ruth was not interested in placing the ball to get to first base. He was trying to knock it out of the park and into the darkness. 'I swing big, with everything I've got,' he said, 'I hit big or I miss big.' Few could swing with anything like the speed Ruth could and, significantly, he began the fashion for lighter bats with thinner handles, marking the demise of hickory.

From the 1930s to the 1990s, ash was the only timber used in professional bat manufacturing. Even during the late 1950s, when a pathogenic fungus began to attack and kill ash trees in New York State, causing great alarm about the longevity of the species, no alternative was adopted. Ash was *the* constant in a game that quietly evolved in many other ways. Of the 1,900-plus bats in the wonderful National Baseball Hall of Fame and Museum in Cooperstown, New York, some 95 per cent are ash.

The supremacy of white ash continued into the new millennium. It remained unchallenged as the timber of choice for the vast majority of pro baseball players until the 2001 season, when the controversial Barry Bonds of the San Francisco Giants broke the single-season home run record, hitting seventy-three 'homers' by swinging a red-handled, black-barrelled bat made from maple. He started a new craze.

Sugar maple is a native North American species that grows well across the Northeast and much of the Midwest. It produces maple syrup, the beloved breakfast sweetener. The light-coloured, dense timber from sugar maple has been used by cabinet-makers and carpenters for centuries. Early in the twentieth century, sugar maple was tested as a possible alternative timber for baseball bats, but it is tricky to season and so improvements in kiln-drying techniques in the 1990s made it viable for the first time.

Scientists have struggled to find any difference in performance between the two wood species. Players, however, have always loved their bats irrationally: in fact, no other professional sportsmen are quite so fussy, superstitious and illogical about their equipment. Today, maple is popular: some 50 per cent of Major League players swing a maple stick; the other half has remained loyal to ash. The surge in the popularity of maple during the first decade of the twenty-first century was not without controversy, however.

All wooden baseball bats are liable to break, but maple and ash bats break in different ways. Ash tends to crack and flake in small pieces. Maple tends to fracture in bigger, jagged shards, sometimes sending fragments tomahawking through the air. In several instances, razor-sharp projectiles from exploding maple bats have been launched at fielders, into the players' dugouts and even into the stands during games, causing serious injury.

White ash, like common ash and other trees such as oak and elm, is a 'ring-porous' species: in each year of growth there are clear concentrations of the two different types of tubular vessels (called xylem) that a tree creates annually. The xylem, known as earlywood, which the tree makes in spring when it is growing fast and requires more water and minerals to be carried to the developing leaves, contains larger, thinner-walled tube cells which are characteristically lighter in colour. The second part of the annual growth cycle is the latewood, when growth slows down: the latewood cells are narrower, thicker-walled and darker. Together, the lighter and darker forms of xylem make up the annual, concentric growth rings – rings that are so agreeably pronounced in ash.

Because of the concentration of these two different types of cells, ash wood has weaker regions, which is why it cleaves so well, as we saw in an earlier chapter. It is also why, when an ash bat strikes a ball repeatedly, the weaker cell walls of the earlywood can collapse. The barrel of the bat starts to soften, the annual rings begin to separate and thin layers begin to flake off. The same cell structure that makes ash prone to flaking also, significantly, channels any cracks that might occur on striking a ball along the length of the bat, ensuring the crack has a long way to go before the bat can actually break in two. This is called ductile-breakage. Crucially, baseball players tend to feel a crack, or at least notice the flaking, and they will retire that bat before it breaks.

Maple, on the other hand, is a 'diffuse-porous' wood: the pores are approximately the same size and distributed evenly throughout each growth ring, and there is no distinction between earlywood and latewood. Thus, there are no weaker regions and flaking does not occur. Cracks can spread in any direction, making maple bats more likely to snap spectacularly, sending fragments flying off at great speed in unexpected directions. Physicists refer to this as 'tensile-breakage'.

There is another, related difference between ash and maple timber, which also helps explain the higher incidence of exploding maple bats. One aspect of wood that has an overwhelming effect on strength is called 'slope of grain' – a wood industry term and a measurement of the angle at which a piece of wood is cut out of a log. It quantifies how straight the grain is along the edge (radial) and flat (tangential) faces of a piece of wood. Put another way, it quantifies how close to parallel a piece of wood is cut with respect to the main axis of wood cells in a tree. When a piece of wood is cut perfectly parallel to the direction of the grain, it will retain the highest strength. Correspondingly, when a piece of wood is cut at an angle to the grain direction, strength diminishes and it is more likely to break.

A piece of wood sawn with a 10-degree slope of grain has around 30 per cent of the strength of a piece cut with the grain running perfectly straight through it. So a baseball bat cut perfectly parallel to the grain direction of the tree will be stronger, and less likely to break, than one that isn't. Of course, it is much easier to cut it parallel to the grain if you can see the grain clearly. Because the lighter and darker forms of early wood and latewood are so pronounced in ash wood, it happens to be very easy to see the grain, and thus determine its direction with the naked eye. With maple, it is much harder to determine the true grain direction by sight alone.

'The Broken Bat Study' produced by the Major League Baseball's Safety and Health Advisory Committee, at a cost of $500,000, investigated why maple bats were shattering in such a spectacular way, and at such an alarming rate. The study led to changes in the 2009 Bat Supplier Regulations. These have done a good deal to iron out faults in the production of maple baseball bats. The number of 'multiple-piece' failure breakages is, happily, now few. Maple continues to provide a fashionable alternative to ash in the professional leagues, even if the employees at Hillerich & Bradsby's sawmills particularly hate processing it.

'We first tried maple decades ago and nobody wanted it, but here we are now. Maple's popular, so we saw it up too. It makes the place stink different, though, and it goes right through the saws, so you're always sharpening. We prefer the smell of the ash. It's a good smell. The ash is kind,' Jeff Eckman, the saw-mill manager said. Dressed in a peaked cap, a camouflage jacket, jeans and black, steel-toe-capped boots, Jeff looked like a woodsman. He had been working at this mill since 1975, but he'd been involved in timber all his life. 'I grew up on a farm right around here,' Jeff said. 'I've never gone far.' He spoke slowly and with intimacy, often pausing between sentences to lift the peaked cap from his head with a lean hand, and reset it. He talked about the mechanization of the logging industry and how this has depleted the skills and knowledge of the loggers. He reminded me a little of a character from the film *The Deer Hunter*. If Nick, played by Christopher Walken, hadn't blown his head off playing Russian roulette in a gambling den in Saigon, he might have ended up working at a sawmill deep in the Allegheny Mountains.

Jeff recalled the time when Hillerich & Bradsby used to make ice hockey sticks and furniture parts, as well as baseball bats, all from ash. He told me how plenty of good ash went down the road to Jamestown, a national centre for furniture-making from the time the early Swedish settlers arrived with their woodworking skills, until twenty years ago. 'It was high-end furniture but nobody wants that anymore. People buy plywood furniture and then when they move house, they throw it away. Nobody cares about the heritage anymore. Ah, it changes,' Jeff said, staring out of the window of the sawmill office, towards the hills where the afternoon sunlight was slowly turning golden.

'We've tried pretty much every native timber to make baseball bats. We've tried aspen, black cherry, Northern red oak, hemlock, hickory, beech and birch. We make a few bats from birch now. A few years ago, we thought every bat would be made from either maple or birch by now. When the emerald ash borer hit, we thought the ash was done for.'

American scientists first officially identified the emerald ash borer (*Agrilus planipennis* Fairmaire), a green-winged, half-inch long, torpedo-shaped beetle, near Detroit, Michigan, in summer 2002. In 2003, the emerald ash borer was detected near Toledo, Ohio. By 2007, ash trees in Illinois, Indiana and Maryland were affected. At the beginning of 2010, the infestation covered an area of over 100,000 square miles across twelve states. By mid-2012, damage had been wrought in sixteen states of the USA and two Canadian provinces. In May 2013, the emerald ash borer arrived in the same New York county as Cooperstown, home to the National Baseball Hall of Fame.

It is hard to comprehend the damage. Since its discovery, this voracious beetle has killed tens of millions of ash trees in North America and the havoc continues to mount. There are several theories on how the beetle was introduced into the USA: most likely, it arrived in a piece of wooden packing material commonly used to ship consumer goods from Asia, where tree species have co-evolved with the beetle over a long time and are resistant to it.

When I first read about the part ash has played in the story of the baseball bat, I wanted to visit the USA. I had initially hoped to carry a stave of my tree to the factory in Louisville, to be turned on a lathe into a beautiful bat. We don't yet have the emerald ash borer in the UK, but I realized, reading about 'the green menace', that it would be insensitive to import a piece of ash, drive several thousand miles around the country with it in my car boot, and then take it home.

The deadly vigour of the emerald ash borer has, incidentally, allowed scientists in some fields to view the relationship between humans and trees in a new light. A US Department of Agriculture Forest Service survey of mortality rates in counties affected by the beetle noted an increase in the frequency of death by cardiovascular and lower-respiratory-tract illnesses. We should be cautious about reading too much into this, because the survey was small and controlling for demographic factors is complicated. However, it is a reminder that the concord between trees and human health is nuanced in many ways, ways that we often fail to acknowledge today, even though the likes of Henry David Thoreau were writing about them 150 years ago, and William Wordsworth sixty years before that.

As we were talking about the emerald ash borer, Jeff opened a drawer in his desk and withdrew two leaflets and a laminated, luggage-label-size card. He glanced at them briefly and handed them to me. The card showed actual-size photos of larvae and adult beetles. The leaflets contained information on the life cycle of the emerald ash borer and the symptoms of infestation of trees, as well as stern warnings about the movement of firewood.

'Take 'em, Rob. You need to know all about it too. It'll be in Britain some day soon, I guess. The authorities here did a good job getting information about the ash borer out. It first got down into southern Pennsylvania six years ago – and we thought then that there'd be no ash left here by now. No ash, huh? It was a big concern, but somehow it has not found its way into these woods, at least not yet,' Jeff said, raising a hand towards the window and the silent forests beyond. 'The ash borer can only fly about a half mile a year. As long as no one takes the beetle and drives it into the centre of the woods, then, you know . . . I'm more optimistic than I was, but can I sit here and say for sure that twenty years from now there'll still be loads of ash round here? No, I can't. It would be a terrible thing to lose it.'

There was a knock and the door to the office swung wide open. A glint-eyed, bright-faced lady in her seventies stood smiling at us. 'You boys hiring?' she said. Laughter cut through the still air and we rose to our feet. Jeff and I walked outside to the row of trucks parked on the grass beside the single-track road. The last, lambent light of the day was brushing the forest canopy on the far hills. The temperature had dropped; there was a hint of winter.

Jeff breathed deeply. He raised and reset his baseball cap again. 'Right where we live here, right in this area, in the Allegheny Mountains and on the Appalachian plateau, this is not just where the best ash comes from, it's where the best timber comes from. This is the best hardwood timber in the world. It's why your people came here in the first place, Rob.'

Finding new sources of wood has been an important cause of population movements, and the rise and fall of civilizations, throughout human history. For at least 5,000 years, from the Bronze Age to the middle of the nineteenth century, the human race has relied on trees as the principal source of fuel and building materials. Time and again, societies have fallen out of sync with nature's patient operation, though: they have exhausted their own forests at home and then had to search for a timber supply elsewhere. The Greeks inadvertently turned the thickly forested but periphery state of Macedon into an economic, and then military power, by buying up all their timber, when Greece had consumed its own. Macedon came to dominate the entire Hellenic world in the fourth century BC. Three hundred years later, the Romans colonized Gaul and Spain partly to access the forests in order to provide timber for industry at home in Italy.

In the seventeenth century, North America's untouched forests were, along with religious freedom, central to its allure to Europeans, especially the English. The first European explorers to reach the north-east coast of America were confronted with 'an interminable wall of forest from their ships, a vastness of untouched primeval splendour', wrote Rutherford Platt in *The Great American Forest* (1965). Certainly nothing like it existed in England, nor had it for at least a millennium. This forest stretched almost unbroken from the Atlantic

Ocean to the Mississippi River and from Maine to Georgia. Though the Pilgrim Fathers at Plymouth Colony initially settled on Indian corn fields in 1620, the forest contributed significantly to the sense of economic optimism from early on: the first return cargo, sent home to the motherland, contained timber. Through felling and exporting the forest, New England was later able to establish itself as one of the wealthiest colonies in the New World.

The majority of early settlers stayed close to the shore. A few, however, struck out west. This great deciduous forest, burgeoning with game and criss-crossed with the tracks of Native American tribes, became the home of the backwoodsman pioneer – and part of the American biography. The pioneer swung his felling axe and in making a clearing in the forest, he provided timber for a log cabin as well as furniture, fencing and tools. Often the first building to be erected after the makeshift cabin, at a clearing on a river, was a sawmill, which provided boards for export to Europe and an income.

The hardwood trees surrounding these backwoodsmen provided a variety of beautifully grained woods with distinct properties. Some were familiar to the European woodsmen; others they learnt about from the Native Americans: the Iroquois, for example, fashioned pipe stems, lacrosse sticks, bows, arrows, baskets and the frames of snowshoes out of white ash. Settlers turned oak and maple into tables and chairs. Straight-grained timbers like poplar and ash were easily worked. Hickory was durable but hard to split. Birch and cherry were good to cook on while oak and crab apple burnt well on the fire, and willow made good charcoal. Tough and elastic, ash made the best rakes, ladders and hoes.

Despite the scale of this forest, who had the right to cut down the trees soon became an issue. From the earliest period of colonization, the English Crown took America's best trees for itself, by custom. After 1691, the finest timber was reserved by law for the exclusive use of the Royal Navy. Of particular interest to the Royal Navy were the eastern white pine trees, which grew up to 300 feet tall and made superb masts. The King's Surveyor of Pines and Timber stalked through this wooded wilderness and marked the best trees with the royal sign – the Broad Arrow, a series of three hatchet slashes. Throughout the early 1700s, resentment over who owned the timber grew among the colonists. Naturally of a dissenting disposition, and now far enough away in time and distance from the old tyrannies and prejudices of the mother country, the colonists regularly cut the marked trees down. Skirmishes with the British authorities followed. Some historians believe that ownership of the trees was as instrumental as taxation on tea in raising the cries for political representation that brought about the American Revolution.

Following American Independence, pioneers continued to advance further into the depths of the Appalachian forest. The timber they extracted was used to make wagons, axles, wheels and bridges, as well as furniture and tools. Villages were commonly built at a waterfall powerful enough to run a sawmill. Shipbuilding became a mainstay of the New England economy. Steamboats on the major rivers were made of and powered by wood and wood remained the primary house-building material until the 1880s. Even railroad tracks were made of wood, while trains were powered by wood up to the Civil War.

In his seminal work on pioneer society, *Statistics of the West, at the Close of the Year 1836*, James Hall called America 'a wooden society'. The practical association with and knowledge of trees was a reality, not just for the first few years following colonization, but for the first 250 years of American history – effectively from the settlement of New England to the popularization of baseball in the late nineteenth century. Yet the forest was not just a physical resource: it was also the environment where, some have argued, the dynamism of the American character was forged.

The historian Frederick Jackson Turner advanced his influential 'frontier thesis' in an essay entitled 'The Significance of the Frontier in American History', first delivered at an exposition in 1892, to celebrate the 400th anniversary of Columbus's arrival in the Americas. He wrote: 'American democracy was born of no theorist's dream; it was not carried in the *Sarah Constant* to Virginia, nor in the *Mayflower* to Plymouth. It came out of the American forest, and it gained new strength each time it touched a new frontier.' Turner believed that the American intellect owed its defining characteristics – 'coarseness and strength combined with acuteness and inquisitiveness, that practical, inventive turn of mind . . . that masterful grasp of material things, lacking in the artistic but powerful to effect great ends, that restless, nervous energy, that dominant individualism . . . and withal that buoyancy and exuberance which comes with freedom' – to the frontiersman who edged tree by tree, clearing by clearing and farm by farm through the great American forest from the Atlantic Ocean to the Mississippi.

Many historians have subsequently rejected Turner's 'frontier thesis', but it does highlight the underlying importance of forests, trees and wood as the nation took shape. During the second half of the nineteenth century, America grew into a great nation and wood was, again, central to that story. Timber barons, railroad trusts and mining companies mowed down vast swathes of mature timber to feed the nation's hunger for wood products like housing, railroad sleepers or ties, pit props and fuel.

The scientist and 'Father of the U. S. Weather Service', Increase Lapham, noted in 1867: 'Without the fuel, the buildings, the fences, furniture . . . utensils and machines of every kind, the principal materials of which are taken directly from the forests, we should be reduced to a condition of destitution.' Cheap timber and fuel were, Lapham felt, crucial factors in America's prosperity. He was also one of the first Americans to comment on the alarming deterioration of America's woodlands, though his warnings went unheard until 1905, when the naturalist President Theodore Roosevelt brought what remained of the nation's forest reserves under the control of the Department of Agriculture.

When Henry David Thoreau went to live 'in the woods, a mile from any neighbour', on the shore of Walden Pond outside Concord, Massachusetts, in 1845, much of the impenetrable forest that once stretched from the Atlantic to the Mississippi had already been cleared. Convinced that 'the mass of men lead lives of quiet desperation', Thoreau moved to the woods for two years and two months 'to front only the essential facts of life,' and emancipate himself from material possessions. Like the early pioneers, he built himself a wooden cabin and furniture using what the forest provided. Thoreau did not do this from necessity, though. He lived like this as an intellectual exercise – to examine the nature of America's first promise, the promise of a new way of dwelling on earth, the promise of an experiment in independence on a richly wooded land.

The wooden cabin at Walden was a symbol of the America that was once on offer, but which it failed to become. Driving away from the sawmill, through the last vestiges of the great Appalachian forest, following the setting sun in the direction of the Mississippi River, I couldn't help but wonder if the ash baseball bat was another symbol of this broken contract, the last shred of a pre-nuptial agreement between humans and the trees that has been almost completely torn to pieces. The forest that confronted the Pilgrim Fathers as they stepped off the *Mayflower* was, many believe, the greatest stand of deciduous, hardwood timber the earth has ever known. And it's nearly all gone.

'The wooden bat is part of the heritage of the game, and that's very important,' Brian Hillerich told me. We were having a cup of coffee in the factory canteen at Hillerich & Bradsby, the business Brian's great-great-grandfather established beside the Ohio river in Louisville, Kentucky, in the late nineteenth century. Every time the door of the canteen opened, the din of the sanding, sawing, dipping and branding of ash flooded in from the machine shop.

'Technology has meant there are composite bats and light-weight metal bats on the market that outperform wooden bats, but the professional players still have to use wood. To lose the wooden bat would destroy the integrity of the game. The dimensions of the field would have to change, for example, because they are based on human speed and batters striking the ball with wooden bats. For 140 years, the rules have said that the bat must be made of one piece of wood. The rule-makers won't even let us reinforce the handles. They want the bats to break because, well, they broke in the beginning,' Brian said.

Perhaps the major consequence of this continuity is that the delicate balance between hitter and pitcher has changed little over such a long period. Thus, the record books remain relevant: fans today can compare batting-average statistics of contemporary players with the great sluggers of the past, con-necting the stars of the modern, $100 million game with legends like Ted Williams, Joe DiMaggio, Hank Aaron, Babe Ruth, Mickey Mantle, 'Shoeless' Joe Jackson and Ty Cobb, perhaps baseball's greatest ever player.

When aluminium bats first became popular in amateur baseball in the late 1960s, purists of the game complained viscerally. They were particularly appalled by the sound of aluminium striking the leather ball – a modern 'boing', 'bing' or 'ping'. It was a fair complaint. The traditional noise of an ash bat on a leather ball – the ringing 'tock' affectionately called the 'crack of the bat' – has to be one of the finest sounds in sport. No other auditory effect communicates the essence of a game quite so comprehensively and efficiently. For many Americans, it is part of the soundscape of the nation; for others, it is simply the voice of summer.

In the early 1970s, the rise in popularity of metal bats prompted an arms race among manufacturers, to produce bats that performed better and better. Soon enough, it was obvious that metal bats were outperforming wooden ones. The 'sweet spot' – the magic spot on a bat where you get the biggest bang for your buck – can be enlarged on a metal bat, making it easier to get a hit. Because a metal bat is hollow, the ball goes further. Because aluminium bats are lighter, players can swing them faster; players also have more control, so they can swing later.

In 1995, Hillerich & Bradsby sold more aluminium than wooden bats for the first time in its long history. The story was the same for all the major bat manufacturers. The ash baseball bat, it seemed, was heading the way of the ash tennis racket – extinction loomed. However, the highest bastion of the game refused to move with the times. The Rules Committee of Major League Baseball (MLB), the governing body of all levels of professional baseball, including Major League, AAA, AA, A, Rookie and Independent Leagues – refused to change its rules. It still refuses to. All non-wooden bats – including a new arsenal of feather-light bats made from materials like graphite, fibreglass, resin and reinforced ceramic, as well as aluminium – remain illegal in professional baseball.

This confounded me at first. The wooden baseball bat really

ought to be a piece of the American past: a museum artefact, a salvaged object in a Wright Morris painting, leaning against a barn in an otherwise empty Nebraska landscape; or as a metaphor on the porch of a deserted farmhouse, in a Walker Evans photograph. America arguably did more than any other nation during the twentieth century to realize the future through technology, science and engineering. The Atomic Age, the Space Age and the revolution in technology all started here. Yet, at the highest level, the national game is not played with a totem of this scientific progress; instead, professional baseball is played with a fragment from the distant past.

Today, the solid wooden baseball bat is an American archetype, the touchstone of a myth that runs through the annals of the country. To hold a baseball bat is to hold a tool: to raise a baseball bat in the air is to ready yourself for labour, just as a young Abraham Lincoln once raised a broad axe to split fencing rails on a frontier farm in Indiana. The continuity in the shape, material and feel of the wooden baseball bat is a rare thing in modern sport. It is reflected in the historical eloquence and the sense of tradition at ball games, and in the pace and rhythm of the players on the field. It is also reflected in the familial feel of the Louisville Slugger factory, and in the sense of stewardship people like Brian Hillerich and Danny Luckett, Hillerich & Bradsby's longest-serving employee, hold over the bat.

Tall, barrel-chested, with powerful hands and a white beard, Danny has been involved in production for forty-four years and is now head of the professional bat department. 'We've been making ash baseball bats here for 129 years. The bat has changed a bit in that time – the handle has got smaller, say. The game has changed a bit too, but really, what we make now is just the same as back then,' Danny said.

Around us, the commotion of the factory floor was hitting a mid-afternoon peak. Forklift trucks carrying cases of creamy-white, cylindrical tubes of ash darted across the floor. To our right, bats were being flame-tempered, a cosmetic finish that burns the grain on a live gas flame. Several sanding machines, covered in a lustrous film of fine sawdust, were whirring away. A cupping machine was drilling out the ends of bats. Further down the line, racks of bats were being dipped, painted and hung up on 'dip lines'. The aroma of freshly cut ash pervaded. Across the factory, an operator was taking one bat at a time and rolling it under a hot metal plate, branding the smooth timber with the most famous marque in baseball bat history – an engraving that leaves a yellow scorch mark across the grain, bearing the words: 'Louisville Slugger: Made in USA, Louisville, Kentucky.'

Danny now operates the CNC lathe that produces the bespoke bats used in the Major League, the highest echelon of professional baseball. Some players still visit him to discuss the detail of their custom-made bats; most of the time, though, they email their orders and Danny selects their chosen bat model from the 1,000 or so stored in the computer's memory. When the programme is ready, he picks a billet of ash from the extensive racks behind him, examines it one last time, and places it in the lathe. In just a few seconds, a stick of white ash is transformed into an American icon.

Earlier, in the museum next door to the factory, I had

seen the collection of historic bats used by former legends of the game. Because of the lucrative market in baseball memorabilia, some of these bats are now worth huge sums. Aficionados agree that the great Joe DiMaggio's record fifty-six-game hitting streak will never now be broken, because of the specialization of pitchers in the modern era: one of the Louisville Slugger bats he used in that famous streak is in the museum and is valued at $500,000 – a lot of money for a stick of ash once worth pennies.

Danny is the last surviving employee who can still turn bats by hand. He can convert an innocuous cylinder of white ash into a professional bat by mounting it in a lathe, sanding and turning it, smoothing, re-smoothing and checking it with callipers against one of the hundreds of model bats, until it is perfect. Danny learnt to hand-turn from Augie Bickel, who, along with other members of the Bickel family, provide the continuity in a manual skill that connects the present with Hillerich & Bradsby's own creation story. Fritz Bickel, the head-turner for half a century, once said that bat-turning 'is like painting and music. You've either got the exact touch or you haven't.'

Part of that 'touch' is a profound knowledge and understanding of ash. Often the players themselves have it: they can be as sensitive with their bats as a violinist trying to tell the difference between a real and a fake Stradivarius. I had read about Ted Williams, the last batter to average .400 in a season. Nicknamed 'The Thumper', Williams had superb, natural hand-to-eye coordination, and his approach to the game was punctilious. Not only did he practise endlessly, he also took an intense interest in his bats. On visits to the Louisville Slugger factory, he would rummage through great piles of dried ash billets, to select precisely the right ones for his own use. He was known for being able to distinguish bats minutely. Once, Williams was given a selection of bats and he picked out the one bat that was half an ounce heavier than the others; then he picked it out again. It is a level of intimacy with a natural material that few of us can appreciate. Williams was also notoriously distant with other human beings and may well have preferred his beloved bats to people.

'Ash is a wonderful material to work. It has just the right properties, the perfect combination of strength, resilience and density,' Danny told me. 'I particularly like the ash because you know what you're getting with it. Pick it up and you can see the grain. You can see if there are any defects. You know straight away that it's a good, solid piece of wood, or not, and 99 per cent of the time, you're gonna be right. We've done trials with all the likely native American hardwoods and even a few tropical hardwoods, over decades, and we just kept on coming back to ash. The maple is more than a fad, but ash has been a wonderful material from the beginning. Will they still be making baseball bats from ash in fifty years' time? Well, I know I won't be. Unless something dreadful happens to the trees, I reckon others will.'

CHAPTER 9

Green Ebony

'To the woodworker the varied dispositions of wood
are almost human: even in the same species they
differ, some yielding to his wishes as though glad to
co-operate, others stubborn and intractable. The
quality of a tree was remembered to the last
fragment after the bulk of the log had been used.'

Walter Rose, *The Village Carpenter*

Five years ago, I had the steel frame of a bicycle made for me
by a British artisan frame-builder. I wrote then about how we
retain possessions that are well made: over time they grow in
value to us and enrich our lives in minute ways when we use
them. I also wrote that this bicycle was the loveliest thing I
had ever owned. It still is. I ride it all the time and I'll ride it
for the rest of my life. I clean it, maintain it and care for it in
a way that foxes my children. This bicycle has become a tal-
ismanic device; it defines my appreciation of the tradition,
lore and beauty of all bicycles.

A year after the tree was felled, I decided to commission a
piece of bespoke furniture out of my ash. Though my home
was filling up with lovely wares from my tree, I recognized
that something was missing. I wanted a totem, an article that
embodied my reverence not just for my ash tree, but for all

ash trees. It was a big step. I'd never commissioned a piece of furniture before. Actually, I'd never even bought a new piece of furniture before.

I telephoned my friend, Andy Dix. We met a few years ago and have a lot in common: we're about the same age; we live nearby; we share a passion for riding bicycles; we love woodlands and we firmly believe in wood as a renewable material of the future. I also admired the fact that Andy had acted on an urge that many of us feel – the urge to make things with your hands: a decade ago, he abandoned a career as a paper shuffler behind a desk, and retrained as a cabinet-maker. I wanted to commission a desk and I had a strong idea of what it would be. The desk would be for writing; there would be three drawers; I would be able to dismantle it; and I wanted to honour the timber with a simple, contemporary design. I had even noted down some rough dimensions.

'Function first, form follows. If it works and it's well made, there's a good chance it will be elegant by nature,' Andy said. 'I'll do an initial design and send you a plywood model. Then we can look at your ash. We can let the qualities of the wood inform the final design. We can let your tree tell its stories.' Andy gave me a list of the timber he required – six boards in total, all 180 centimetres long and 35 centimetres wide, and in varying thicknesses from 1 to 2 inches.

I delivered the timber to Whitney Sawmills, where it was placed in a kiln to dry for six weeks. When the moisture content was down to 10 per cent, Andy would collect it and we would meet in his workshop to select the wood for each component. Later, Andy emailed 3-D projections of the design.

Shortly after that, a shoebox arrived containing a plywood model of the desk.

My wife, who used to work as a furniture restorer, put the model on the kitchen table and walked around it, sucking her teeth. 'It looks very grand,' she said. 'Was ash traditionally used for solid furniture? Are you sure you shouldn't start with something more modest? What about a chair?'

Of the thousands of village craftsmen who have made traditional, vernacular furniture throughout rural Britain between the Middle Ages and the present, the best known is probably Philip Clissett. Born into a chair-making family in 1817, Clissett, who learnt the craft from his father, made chairs with frames of unseasoned ash turned on a pole lathe at a workshop in the village of Bosbury, Herefordshire, for over sixty years. He was prolific and skilful: he once claimed he could make a chair a day.

The 'frame' chairs Clissett made comprised four posts as legs; the two rear legs extended above the seat and were held together by horizontal components which formed the back of the chair. The seats were either solid wood, usually elm, or fashioned from woven rushes. They belonged to a tradition that dates from the sixteenth century: the numbers of chairs made only proliferated, however, during the eighteenth and nineteenth centuries, as they became affordable first to the lower gentry and, eventually, to artisans and the labouring classes. Although frame chairs are particularly associated with the West Midlands and the North-west of England, they were made almost everywhere at some point.

The majority of turned, frame chairs produced during this period broadly fall into two categories: spindle-back, characterized by various arrangements of vertically aligned spindles in the back of the chair; and ladder-back, made with a series of horizontal, flattened, normally bowed slats that look a bit like the rungs on a ladder. Philip Clissett made both. There was, however, a huge amount of regional variety within these two categories, at least until the homogenization of Britain took off towards the end of the nineteenth century. The chair-makers' minutely different devices, local materials and the numerous variations in the number, size and shape of the slats and spindles, served to accent the chairs in myriad regional ways, like dialects in Britain at one time.

These chairs were not stately pieces of furniture, kept in closed rooms and passed from generation to generation. As so often in the story of man and the ash tree, they were simple items in daily use. Ornamental considerations were secondary; function dominated their form. They were sturdy, utilitarian, domestic artefacts built for the hurly-burly of life in a country kitchen.

In 1801, roughly three quarters of the nine million or so people in Britain still lived in the countryside. Most homes would have had a chair or two. Partly because of their low intrinsic value and partly because antique collectors and historians showed no interest in vernacular furniture until the late twentieth century, only a small number of these frame chairs pre-dating 1850 have survived. The majority would have ended up, once they were beyond repair, on the fire.

This particular chair-making tradition might well have

been forgotten altogether had it not been for a chance encounter in the village of Bosbury in 1886. James MacLaren, a Scottish architect working nearby in Ledbury, took a wrong turning in the village and stumbled across Philip Clissett's workshop. MacLaren was an influential architect and an evangelist of the Arts and Crafts Movement. The Movement, inspired by the writings of John Ruskin and the work of designer William Morris, championed an idealized version of late medieval life, and thereby the virtues of craftsmanship, as a counterpoint to the machine age and mass production taking over Britain in the late nineteenth century.

MacLaren was struck by Clissett's simple, brick workshop. Everything about it appealed: the pole lathe, the piles of locally sourced, unseasoned ash logs, the authenticity of the process, the tradition and the sincerity of a product that reflected the ideals of the maker. Alfred Powell, another Arts and Crafts luminary, later described a visit to Bosbury, perhaps romantically, as a 'glimpse of what the old aristocratic poor used to be'.

Bernard Cotton, author of *The English Regional Chair*, described the meeting between Clissett and MacLaren as 'a seminal point in the subsequent development of the Arts and Crafts Movement'. The ladder-back chair was the physical embodiment of many ideals the Movement was trying to promote. MacLaren, who had some experience of furniture design, tinkered with a Clissett original and then commissioned him to make eighty or so chairs for the nascent Art Workers' Guild in Bloomsbury, London. These chairs are still in use in the Guild's meeting hall today.

Devotees saw the chairs in Bloomsbury and duly made the pilgrimage to Bosbury. Further large-scale commissions followed for Clissett. William Morris designed and sold a range of rush-seated, ash ladder-back chairs. Charles Rennie Mackintosh used Clissett chairs in his early commissions. Many adherents of the Movement furnished their homes with them.

Ernest Gimson, a prominent furniture designer and later founder of one of the most important branches of the whole Arts and Crafts Movement, the Cotswold School, spent six weeks in Bosbury learning how to make chairs with Clissett in 1890. Gimson, convinced that honest work produced artefacts free from fakery, set up his own furniture business in Gloucestershire in 1902. He employed Edward Gardiner, who later moved his chair-making workshop to Warwickshire, where Neville Neal joined him as an apprentice in 1939. Today, Neville's son Lawrence still makes chairs by hand from local coppiced ash, providing the continuity in a traditional use of ash that stretches back, unbroken, to the late Middle Ages.

Clissett died in 1913, aged ninety-six. He is buried in an unmarked grave in Bosbury churchyard. His life still serves as a model for country craftsmen. His chairs – simple, dignified, with rush seats and turned, steam-bent ash components – are collected by museums on both sides of the Atlantic.

My parents had an ash ladder-back chair with a woven rush seat. It was a rocking chair, sometimes known as a nursing chair, given to my mum by my grandmother when my brother was born. When I was a kid, I idled in it for hours. It has been repaired several times and my brother still has it today.

Frame chairs were not exclusively produced from ash, but

wherever it grew well, it was the material of choice: it was cheap and available, fast growing, readily cleaved, easily bent, light, strong and elastic enough to take the bashes and crashes of daily life. As my wife correctly suspected, though, ash was never a popular choice in the manufacture of solid furniture. In fact, I couldn't find a single historical record of an ash desk.

'It is curious,' Andy said, leading me into his workshop. 'Generally speaking, common ash is regarded as a species with good to excellent working properties. It makes great furniture. I don't know why it hasn't been used for desks.'

'Working properties' is an umbrella term woodworkers use to cover the characteristics and behaviour of different species. It encompasses how particular woods saw, glue, take preservatives, turn, sand, and hold nails and screws. Green ash, Andy explained, has a mild tendency to catch the teeth of the saw when it's being cut, but seasoned ash is easily sawn, planed and sanded to a smooth, clean surface. Ash glues well. It can also be readily polished, stained and varnished. There are weaknesses, though – ash holds nails poorly and it is hard to impregnate with preservatives (which makes it a poor choice for outdoor furniture) – but all in all, ash yields an end product with great strength relative to its weight and the amount of energy expended to shape it.

Andy's workshop is a wooden shed on the edge of a village, hidden away in a part of Herefordshire that remains deeply rural. Philip Clissett would have approved. I had followed a lattice of lanes and taken several wrong turns at junctions without signposts, trying to find it. A horseshoe was nailed to the door. Inside, the wood-burning stove had created a thick fug. The walls were covered with shelves stacked with wane-edge Western red cedar boards and sawn blocks of oak. Andy had a collection of modern machines and tools, but there was also a rack of old wood-turning chisels. Centre stage was the piece of furniture Andy had just finished – a magnificent pedestal desk made from walnut.

'It's good that you're here today,' Andy said, clearing a workbench. 'We can choose the wood for the writing surface together. It's interesting, your timber. There is no distinction between the sapwood and the heartwood of your tree, but there is a dramatic change where the wood colours in the middle. They could be two different trees.'

The coloured wood, often known as olive ash and common in old ash trees, is caused by the build-up of pigmented material that works its way into the dead cells close to the centre of the tree. According to John Evelyn, it was highly valued in the seventeenth century, when woodworkers called coloured ash 'green Ebony'. Andy explained how the legs would all come from the light, typically creamy-white wood; the back of the desk and the side pieces around the surface would be in the darker brown wood, from the heart of the tree; the three drawer-fronts would be light-coloured, in contrast to the darker pieces that separated them. 'That makes sense of the tree. We don't want to over-complicate it,' Andy said. Together we manoeuvred the boards around the machinery and onto the main workbench.

Perhaps the most important design consideration with wooden furniture is allowing for any movement in the wood:

movement can occur following changes in the temperature and humidity in the environment where the furniture lives, Andy explained. Wood remains hygroscopic – it is constantly trying to attain a state of equilibrium with the air surrounding it – for ever. The trick is to make sure any movement pursuant to a change in the moisture content in the wood, for example when the piece is moved from the workshop to the client's centrally heated home, will be swallowed by the structure, without splitting any components. Andy wanted to create the writing surface out of two different boards, by sawing or 'ripping' one wide board into two pieces and inserting another piece, from a different part of the tree, into the middle. 'This way we can reverse the direction of the grain in the middle piece. When moisture is taken up by this top surface as a whole, the outside sections will want to cup or curve in one direction and the middle piece will want to curve in the other direction. To a large extent, they'll cancel each other out,' Andy said.

There was one obvious candidate for the 1-inch-thick board that would be ripped down the middle. At the sides of this board, the wood was creamy and pale with arrow-straight, parallel lines of grain. As there was some coloration in the middle of the wood – a gentle fade from creamy-white through camel to cappuccino – Andy wanted to find a centre piece that picked up that change, so that the hue would flow from light to dark to light again across the whole writing surface. He also wanted to find the piece of timber with the most interesting 'figure'.

Woodworkers use the term 'figure' to collectively describe

the markings on the surfaces of wood. Figure is the result of a combination of all the anatomical features, from normal wood structure, including growth rings, to various abnormalities like knots. Generally, the more inconsistent the grain and the greater the frequency of abnormalities, the more pronounced the figure is. Figure comes in innumerable forms, many of which are distinctive and characteristic of particular tree species. Woodworkers have a delightful vocabulary of words and phrases to describe figure: ribbon, bird's eye, flame, fiddleback, quilted, blistered, stripe, broken stripe and dimpling figure are just a few.

'We're looking for any eye-catching details like swirling grain, knots, evidence of any traumas the tree suffered long ago and for abnormalities in growth,' Andy said, levering a piece of timber out. It was a 10-inch-wide, 6-foot-long board of discoloured wood from the centre of my tree. There was detail in the figure, but it was difficult to make out. Andy said it was a carpenter's hunch at this point: passing the board through the thicknessing machine would make the figure more visible, by neatly cutting the fibres that had previously been roughly torn by the saw at the sawmill.

'Looking at a rough-sawn board is a bit like looking at the surface of water riffled by wind. You only get the vaguest impression of what lies beneath. Pass that board over a planer, though, and it's like looking into the water through a glass-bottom bucket,' Andy said.

The transformation was extraordinary. The machine took a layer of skin off both sides of the board to reveal what was once the dynamic internal system of the tree. There was plenty of interesting detail and variation. Andy passed it through the thicknessing machine again: the figure was even more clearly defined, like a body-builder tensing his forearm to lift the veins. The texture, hue and colour of this board would perfectly complement the one we had already selected.

Andy ran his hand across the wood. He looked boyish and animated. So much of cabinet-making is about engineering, albeit with one of nature's gifts: it is about understanding the different species of wood; knowing their load-bearing capacities, stability and resistance to rot; it is about real knowledge gained by solving real problems. Yet there is also an aesthetic allure in almost every piece of wood.

While the kettle was boiling, Andy explained the next part of the process. The last of the components, including the boards for the writing surface, would be cut out, jointed and dry-assembled. The desk would be left for a further week, to see if there was any movement. Everything would then be taken apart, dimensioned precisely, jointed again, sanded and finished.

The desk was delivered in parts, a few weeks later, on a sparkling spring day. My wife helped me carry the components down to my office. With Andy's notes, the desk was easily assembled. We lifted it gingerly into place, in front of the window facing the stream and the woodland on the opposite bank. I pulled a chair up and placed the palms of my hands reverentially on the writing surface.

'I think I'll leave you two alone for a while,' my wife said, stepping outside into the sunlight.

I had a bespoke writing desk. It was an extravagance – but it was also original, authentic, repairable and very good value. With no employees to pay and minimal overheads, Andy was able to charge me a fair price. Every component had been designed, considered, sawn, planed, roughed out and finished individually. In its entirety, the desk testified to the skill, judgement, honesty and integrity of the maker; to the years he spent learning his craft, and to his relationship with the wood. It was beautiful.

I opened one of the drawers and got a waft of freshly sawn ash. The odour took me straight back to Callow Hill Wood and the day the tree was felled. I inhaled another nose-full of the distinctive smell: it had been a thread running through the whole journey. I drank it in again and thought of John and Michael in the tool-handle factory, of Phill cutting felloes, of Robin's medieval bowl-turning workshop, of Tom shaving curls of ash from an arrow shaft, of Christian and Thomas steam-bending the runners of my toboggan, of the boys buying their first hurleys in Frank's workshop, and of Danny feeding creamy-white billets of ash into a lathe in Louisville, Kentucky. Andy had told me that the smell of the timber would linger in the drawers for months, possibly years. Each time I reached in for a pencil or an envelope, I would have a moment of sensory nostalgia, a kind of communion with all the people who had helped me with my ash tree.

The desk had been finished with a hard-wearing wax. The writing surface was tactile and almost three-dimensional. When the wind blew outside, the sunlight shimmered through the trees and refracted off the desktop, producing an almost holographic effect. The straight grain in the pale wood on the edges of the surface contrasted dramatically with the meandering ripples and swirls in the dark wood. There, the grain shifted like eddies of smoke in the wind. There were knots, variegated pools and specks of even darker wood, which gathered in clusters called 'cat's paws'. It was transfixing.

When I rang Andy to thank him, he said: 'The desk is coherent as a piece of furniture because it's all from the same tree, and because the ash itself has made some of the decisions. Knowing the history of your tree and where it comes from, just down the road here, I have been looking at it more closely. All the tiny elements of figure and the variety in colouring have prompted me to consider the growing process in more detail – at least when the radio is broken I do. Anyway, it's done. You'd better write a book now.'

With Gentle Hand Touch

On a bright morning at the end of winter, with a keen wind blowing out of the north-west, I returned to Callow Hill Wood. It was almost two years since my first visit – the day I found my tree. From the corner of the wood, I walked up the sunken track. A buzzard started from a high branch. My spaniels put a cock pheasant up. The winter sunlight angled in through the trees, painting filaments of gold on the carpet of decaying leaves. Near the top of the hill, kids had built a mountain-bike track in and out of the scooped earth, where limestone was once quarried. Several trees, probably victims of the autumnal storms, were hanging in the branches of their neighbours.

In the clearings and along the edges of the paths, thousands of ash seedlings sprouted from the ground in great clumps. On the northern boundary, where the conifers had been cleared a few years ago, the ash saplings had shot up. I looked for signs of ash dieback, and found none. With such vigorous and profuse natural regeneration, it is hard to believe that the ash tree is under threat. Yet it is.

You won't read about Callow Hill Wood in scholarly books on the British countryside. It is neither important nor noteworthy. It's just a regular gathering of trees 'dreaming out their old stories to the wind', as Thomas Gray wrote; it's a footnote in the antique story of the British landscape. Yet, like thousands of similarly anonymous, small woodlands across the land, it is special. It is a conflicting and harmonious pool of natural life, a mix of the timeless and the evanescent, and a marriage of the utilitarian and the heart-stoppingly exquisite.

Walk fifty paces into a wood and there is a sense of things being different: you are cut adrift. Woods are bewitching places, exuding confidence and calm. They invite introspection. I first became interested in woodlands when I moved to this part of the country. Determined not to live like a refugee in my own landscape, I wanted to understand some of the traditions that make up the inheritance of rural culture, before they are gone for ever. I also wanted to get closer to the nature that surrounds me. Trees, it seems to me, summon us to witness nature; they are closest to its heart.

A few years ago my father died suddenly, at the beginning of winter. For a while after his death I hated being inside: I could feel the shock reverberating within the walls. Working in the woods through that winter gave me the space and time to grieve. I spent hours sitting among the trees waiting for the immemorial stirrings of spring. I enjoyed the solitude, though I never felt truly alone. Trees mark the passing of time in their seasonal change. This reminds us that life passes too, which encourages us to live it as well as we can.

Dad always preferred books to billhooks, but I did wonder if I was encountering his soul sometimes, lingering among the trees, to guide me through the dark forest of loss. When spring arrived, though, I knew the meditative work of stacking timber and piling up brash had whittled away at my grief.

Meanwhile, a feeling that one is sometimes overcome by in woodlands, a hair-raising, transcendent sense that is as common as it is precious and which I couldn't account for, had grown in strength. I now believe that this feeling is the spirit of all the people who have ever known the woods; it's a force representing the continuity in the intense and mutually beneficial relationship between people and trees over the ages; it's a siren song to one of the oldest and deepest connections to the land, and nature, that humans have. Our woodlands are the result of the interaction of humans and natural processes over millennia. We are bound to them, even if we don't know it. At the heart of that bond is the story of man's quotidian relationship with the ash tree.

I reached the glade where my tree had stood and sat down on the stump. Two dozen new shoots of ash, already 3 foot long, were growing out of the edge of the stump: there was life in the tree yet. I could see the sun rising on the dewy field beyond the wood, illuminating a million pearls of moisture suspended from the tip of every blade of grass. When the sun broke through a gap in the trees, I raised my head and let the light burn golden palaces onto my closed eyelids.

The dogs leapt onto the stump behind me and took turns lapping up the rainwater out of the rotten hole in the centre. A drinking vessel – could that be counted as one of the uses of my tree? Perhaps not. Certainly, the brash and the branches that I had left in piles around the stump could be. Then there was the pile of firewood at home, the wooden bowls, the wheel felloes, the arrow shafts, a selection of tool handles, a toboggan and a desk. That wasn't the end of it, though. It was hardly the beginning. I got my notebook out. How many different uses had I actually got from one tree?

On a glorious day in high summer, a few months after the tree was felled, I took a log deep into the Herefordshire countryside, to be cleaved into tent pegs at H. W. Morgan and Sons, one of the last traditional tent peg-makers in Britain. Philip and Glyn Morgan inherited the business their father and uncle set up in 1968, originally making ash bends for hockey sticks and producing tent pegs. Philip and Glyn produce 80,000 to 100,000 hand-cleaved ash tent pegs a year. On a good day, they can make up to 800 each. The economy of effort and the speed at which they worked, even while they were talking to me, was extraordinary. Within minutes, there was a pile of nineteen 12-inch ash pegs on the floor. The brothers refused to take any money from me, and they sent me away with my pegs and a bin liner of ash shavings – the by-product of peg-making. 'They're the best firelighters in the world,' Philip said.

Jonty Hampson and Sascha Gravenstein, together known as Hampson Woods, took three offcuts from planks that had been sawn up to specific dimensions for other uses. Jonty is a carpenter, while Sascha has a background in fine art and design. They make a range of quirky but simple, thoughtfully designed, craft-driven homeware from British timber in an East London workshop. They had not had much experience working with ash, but they liked the idea of getting as many uses out of my tree as possible. They are also interested in the provenance of the wood they use. When we first spoke on the phone, I recognized two young men who were gently trying to make the world more intelligible by bringing the origin of everyday things closer to home.

'People's emotional response to wood is different to other materials. We see this when we sell our stuff at street markets. Everyone wants to touch and smell the things we make,' Sascha said, when I went to collect the wares. They had converted my scraps of ash into seven chopping boards of various sizes, four porridge spoons and a large jam spoon. Each piece managed to articulate something about my tree. 'We didn't appreciate the amazing range in colouring until we started to saw your ash. The smell is great too. Above all, though, it's so nice to work, for a hardwood. It's . . . I don't know, somehow buttery. We'll use ash more in the future,' Jonty said.

The timber stack in my barn was severely depleted when I first heard about Tim Rowe of Edenwood Paddles. Tim hand-crafts bespoke canoe paddles from a variety of wood species, including ash, in a workshop in Cumbria. His paddles, based on old Native American designs, sell all over the world. Tim was exacting on the quality and precise in the dimensions of the timber he required to make me a paddle. My last plank from Whitney Sawmills – a clean, classically creamy-white, 1-inch board from near the outside of the trunk with straight grain – just met the requirements. I couriered it north. Six weeks later a box arrived. I had no idea a simple canoe paddle could be so arrestingly beautiful. It was made to fit me, and felt like it. Instinctively, I knew I would have it for the rest of my life.

When I had finished thumbing through my notebook,

I counted up all the different uses: the grand total was forty-four. I had gathered an extraordinary horde of artefacts and wares that I would cherish for decades – from one tree. Many of them – the kitchen worktops, benches, bowls, spatulas, spoons and chopping boards – were already in daily use. They were scuffed and scratched and quietly radiating their significance throughout my home. Others, like the toboggan and the paddle, were patiently waiting for their moment. Some of the artefacts had a distant future, I reflected, beyond the lives of the craftsmen who made them. The panelling in my office exerted something of the personality of my tree. My desk was a repository of time, a record of the earth's past; in idle moments I studied the grain and wondered at the great winters, long summers, storms and droughts that caused my tree to grow the way it did. Simply holding one of the axe handles was a reminder that the past is not as remote as we think it is.

Individually, the objects spoke of the skill and the idealism of the artisans and craftsmen who had made them, people whose knowledge hinted at a time when the affinity between humans and nature was at a more sensitive pitch. Together, the objects spoke of the long and creative relationship between humankind and ash, an accord of intense intimacy recurring from one civilization to another over millennia. I had felled an ash tree and made best use of it. What could be simpler, I wondered. It had been a deeply satisfying venture that left me feeling rooted to a place in the turning world.

The dogs leapt up and started barking at something moving deeper into the wood. I realized I had been sitting on the stump for an hour. I packed up my flask and notebook. I walked down the hill, out of the wood and into the warm sunshine. The wind, now blowing gently out of the south-west, carried the first hint of spring, a season of hope for nature just as much as for us. I felt sad that my time with this tree was ending. Still, my new rapport with the ash was only just beginning.

Postscript

Chalara fraxinea or ash dieback was first observed in Europe around 1990, in the Baltic states of Latvia and Lithuania. It has since spread to most parts of the Continent, including Great Britain and Ireland. The disease is caused by a microscopic fungus *Hymenoscyphus fraxineus*, commonly known as *Chalara*, which inhabits ash leaves and twigs. In summer, the fungus produces a chemical which is toxic to the tree. In autumn, it produces dust-like spores which spread very efficiently. No one is certain how or even if the fungus was introduced to Europe: it might be a mutation or hybridization of a previously existing fungus, or it may have been inadvertently imported from Asia, where the fungus is known: it has co-evolved with species of ash in Korea and Japan. Its prolific spread across Europe has been substantially aided by man.

Ash dieback has wreaked havoc in many countries: on average, some 70 per cent of trees are infected across continental Europe, with disastrous effect. The symptoms of ash dieback – wilted leaves, dark strips of bark on twigs, diamond-shaped lesions on stems with dead twigs or branches in the middle, and new growth from buds below the dead part – can be hard to diagnose. They are most evident in young trees or coppice shoots, which are more readily affected than older trees. In large ash trees, the process from initial infection to death can take several years, while some *Chalara*-infected trees don't seem to die. There is some natural immunity within ash to the fungus, giving us small cause for hope.

However, there is another, even greater threat to our ash trees which I wrote about in Chapter 8. The emerald ash borer, a voracious and destructive beetle, also originally from Asia where tree species have evolved with it over a long time and are resistant, was first identified in the USA in 2002. It is most likely to have arrived in wooden packing material used to transport goods. It has since killed tens of millions of ash trees across North America.

Susceptibility to the emerald ash borer varies within the different species of ash found in North America, but the beetle will infest them all. White ash is particularly susceptible. According to a 2007 report by the US Department of Agriculture's Animal and Plant Health Inspection Service (APHIS), there are an estimated 7.5 billion ash trees in the timberlands of the USA, plus 30 to 90 million ash trees planted in urban areas. Every one of them is at risk.

The female beetle lays her eggs on an ash tree and the larvae bore through the outer bark to feed on the inner bark and phloem, the vascular tissue that carries sugars and other metabolic products downward from the leaves. Eventually the tree's supply of nutrients is cut off. Fully grown beetles then gnaw their way out in May and move on to attack other ash trees during summer. Trees die within one to three years of being infested with eggs.

The metallic-green beetle can only travel short distances each year, but its spread across North America has been maximized by the movement of ash nursery stock, timber, wood chip and especially firewood. In fact, human behaviour has been a defining factor in the impact of the emerald ash borer. APHIS did establish a federal quarantine on the movement of firewood from any hardwood tree, as well as ash nursery stock, green timber and other materials in 2003, but it seems to have done little to slow the dispersal. In 2008, APHIS issued a regulation requiring the heat treatment of all hard-wood firewood imported from Canada.

Various multi-disciplinary teams of scientists from govern-ment agencies and universities have enacted several ways to stem the impairment of America's ash trees: traps baited with manuka oil, removing the bark or 'girdling' certain ash trees, in the hope the beetle will then leave other trees alone, and traps baited with a synthesis of the adult female ash borer's pheromone, to ensnare males, have all been tried. Three species of parasitic wasps have been imported from north-east Asia and released as biological control agents in several states. These initiatives are all focused on slowing the spread: eradication of the emerald ash borer is no longer regarded as feasible. The use of fungal pathogens is still being evaluated. Seed storage and cryopreservation techniques are also being developed in the aim of ensuring there will be ash trees in the future.

If caught early, an infested ash tree can be saved through the injection of insecticides annually or biennially. This is prohibitively expensive, however, and impractical on a forest scale. In fact, the cost of fighting the emerald ash borer is already huge: according to a 2009 US Department of Agri-culture (USDA) report, federal and state agencies had already spent $209 million trying to control the beetle's impact.

The beetle has more recently been identified in Russia, east

of Moscow. It seems inevitable that it will reach Europe, probably before 2025. Predictions are difficult, but it is reasonable
to assume that the populations of ash in both Europe and
North America, along with a wide array of biodiversity that
depends on the species, will continue to be devastated over
the next half century. Losing ash from the landscape will be
as calamitous as the virtual eradication of elms in Britain by
Dutch elm disease, another fungus, in the 1970s.

The spread of tree pests and pathogens is nothing new. When
international trade increased exponentially in the nineteenth
century, plant and tree blights inevitably followed: pests and
diseases that had co-evolved with species of trees in one place
over time, wreaked havoc when they were introduced to new,
unadapted hosts in other parts of the world. In the early twentieth
century, rich countries instituted bio-security regimes and the
incidence slowed. Across Europe, the infection rate picked up
again around 1970, probably as a result of the effect of economic
integration. Today, the spread of new pests and pathogens around
the world is gathering pace again, as the volume and speed of
international trade and human movement increases. In fact, the
globalization of diseases is now thought to be the greatest threat
to the world's trees and forests, greater even than climate change.

Until recently, ash was considered by many to be a 'tree of
the future'. Unless we are prepared to act now – to improve
plant pathology and international bio-security, initiate meas-
ures that anticipate and protect against new pests and diseases,
stop importing trees in huge numbers, and simply learn to
value our trees again – ash will very likely, at some point in
the twenty-first century, become a tree of the past.

Even ash, I do thee pluck,
Hoping thus to meet good luck.
If no good luck I get from thee,
I shall wish thee on the tree.

Old English rhyme

Inventory

A complete list of everything my ash tree produced (in no particular order):

A desk

A toboggan

Six axe handles

Six maul handles

Eight spoons – hand-carved with a side axe, a chisel and a drawknife by Bart Bagnall, a local green woodworker, from branch wood. These delicate, decorative, beautifully finished spoons are irregularly shaped and subtly variegated, all in their own faded hues of cream and umber.

Ten spatulas – also hewn by Bart Bagnall.

A canoe paddle

A coffee table

A 'triangle' chair – modelled on one from a painting by Pieter Breugel the Elder.

The frames of two landing nets – fashioned by Paul Cook, who makes exquisite, hand-made coarse fishing floats, bespoke cane rods and ash frame landing nets.

Ten three-legged, rustic milking stools – the components were roughed out by Roy Nowicka, a local woodworker, and then assembled by children at our annual community woodland group picnic. The children took them home.

Firewood

Kindling

Charcoal – as a community woodland group, we make charcoal and sell it locally.

A meat-carving board – made by Antony Daniels, a local cabinet-maker: the prototype board is set at an angle on legs, so the juices from the joint being carved run off the narrow end into a vessel below.

A shop counter – Andy Dix, who made my desk, converted a plank left over into a shop counter, for a craft beer store in Hay-on-Wye run by a mutual friend.

A 'wheel' for the roof of a sixteen-foot yurt – two pieces of branch wood were sawn, steam-bent and pegged together by Martin Cook, another local woodworker.

The barrel of an ink pen – Martin Cook turned a small leftover block into the barrel of a fountain pen. The pen sits on my desk. I hadn't used an ink pen for years, but I am now in the habit again.

A set of dominos – made by my old friend, Armando Lopez Garcia, a cabinet-maker and carpenter; he was originally from Cuba, where dominos is a serious business.

Panelling – a pile of the branch wood, originally sawn into planks on the mobile sawmill in Callow Hill Wood, went to the workshop of Phil Noble, a local joiner. The splits were cut out; the planks were sawn to length, planed and finished with tongue and groove, 'pencil mould' edges. There is nine square metres of panelling, covering two walls in my office – it has transformed the room. Phil had taken great care to include as much of the figure as possible: there are knots of many sizes; the grain runs straight through some boards, while it ripples and swirls in others; the cast of the wood runs from cream to cappuccino brown; all the boards are different widths, which adds to the natural feel.

Felloes for cartwheels

Bicycle wheel rims – Phill Gregson, the wheelwright, used the one-inch timber board I gave him to make the wheel rims of a nineteenth-century 'boneshaker' bicycle, which he helped to restore.

Arrow shafts

A set of three wooden bowls

Thirty bookmarks – made by Lisa Standley, who runs a local coppice craft business.

Nineteen tent pegs

Animal bedding – the sawdust from Whitney Sawmills is sold on to farmers and used in livestock sheds.

Cooking fuel – I gave several bags of sawdust, which I collected off the mobile sawmill, to a neighbour who smokes his own bacon and fish at home.

Seven chopping boards

Four porridge spoons

A large jam spoon

Three 'trooks' – individual wooden coat hooks made by Geoff Fisher, an artist, designer and maker in the Chilterns. Geoff makes skipping-rope handles, brush handles, bread platters, whistles, iPod stands and 'bug houses' amongst other items, all from thin branch wood and sticks collected in his local woodlands. His unique products are sold in design shops worldwide.

Two catapults – also made by Geoff Fisher.

A prototype bicycle – five boards of various dimensions went across the country to Michael Thompson, a wooden bicycle designer and builder.

Components of surfboards – James Otter makes surfboards and 'handplanes' used for body surfing out of British timber in Cornwall. Clients on his board building workshops used strips of my ash inserted into the main structure as 'liners', to add strength down the centre of the board where your feet land when you stand up. The light-coloured ash was also employed to contrast with the strips of darker oak and walnut, giving an aesthetic dynamic to the boards.

A refectory table – made by John Spivey, the carpenter in my village.

Two free-standing benches – to go with the refectory table.

Two fixed benches – beside the boot rack in my house.

Two coat racks – waney-edge boards from branch wood, fixed to the wall with hooks screwed in.

Two large kitchen worktops

Shelving – Matthew Plumb, the lumberjack-poet who helped fell my tree, took a six-foot by one-foot board for a shelf in the kitchen of the home he proposes to build on the chassis of an old truck.

The frame of a coracle – Malcolm Rees, a well-known coracle-maker on the river Tywi in Carmarthen, West Wales, used several laths measuring eight foot by one and a quarter inches by three eighths of an inch to form the egg-shaped base of a traditional coracle. These small, lightweight, oval boats have been used for river transport and fishing in Britain since at least Roman times.

A dozen cricket stumps, plus bails

Rotting wood – I left the brash, most of the smaller-diameter branch wood and several larger logs on the floor in Callow Hill Wood, to slowly rot away. Decomposing deadwood is important to many species of insects, fungi, mosses, lichens, invertebrates and small mammals. This wood will rot along with the fallen leaves and eventually return to the earth as humus, the organic component of soil. Decades from now, that humus will encourage ash seeds to become saplings and then trees, in the continual process of death and renewal that is at the heart of the woodland ecosystem.

Go to http://robpenn.net/ash-project/ for more.

Acknowledgements

I am profoundly grateful to all the woodmen, foresters, artisans, friends, craftsmen and makers who have generously shared their expertise and passion for trees and wood. They include Joe Atkinson, Bart Bagnall, Will Bullough, Martin Cook, Paul Cook, Antony Daniels, Andy Dix, Geoff Fisher, Martin Frazer, Christian and Thomas Gasser of Gasser Rodel, Jonty Hampson and Sacha Gravenstein of Hampson Woods, Armando Lopez Garcia, Phill Gregson, John Lloyd of AS Lloyd & Son, James Otter from Otter Surfboards, Tom Mareschall, Philip and Glyn Morgan, Frank Murphy, Liam and Danny Murray of Woodelo Bicycles, Phil Noble, Roy Nowicka, Matthew Plumb, Malcolm Rees, Tim Rowe of Edenwood Paddles, John Spivey, Lisa Standley of Cottage Coppicing, Michael Thompson, Robin Wood and Rob Yorke.

Mark Potter of Abersenny Woodland Management played a key part in helping me find my tree. Without Ed Morell, I wouldn't have spent a wonderful afternoon high up in the canopy of my tree. Jez Ralph of Timber Strategies was my patient guide to the mechanical properties of wood. In Ireland, Sam Beresford, Joe Christle, Hugo Jellett, Marty Mulliga and John Torpey all went out of their way to help. In the USA, Brian Boltz, Matt Bynum, Jeff Eckman, Brian Hillerich, Danny Luckett and Rick Redman, all of Hillerich & Bradsby, as well as Tim Wiles and Freddy Berowski in the

National Baseball Hall of Fame library, kindly gave up their time to talk.

For sharing their knowledge of the ash tree and its many uses, and helping in a multitude of other ways, I am also very grateful to Mike Abbott, George Beane, Jo Binns, Andrew Erskine, Wyndham Morgan, Jake Steel and all the good folk of the Crucorney Woodland Group, Tim Cochrane, Dr Tony Cowell, David Curtis of the Centre for Sports Engineering Research, Dougal Driver and the team at Grown in Britain, Sarah Farmer, Oli Field, Nick Gibbs, Dr Gabriel Hemery and Alistair Yeomans of the Sylva Foundation, Richard Herkes, Pip Howard, David Jenkins, Keith Jones from Forestry Commission England, Gary Kerr and Andrew Price from Forest Research, Thomas Kirisits, Guy Mallinson, Tom and Sara Matson, Dr Daniel Miles, Mark Morgan, Geraint Richards, Stefano Santilli, David Saunders of Woodnet, Cameron Short, James Suter, Phil Tidey at the Small Woods Association, John Toy, Monica Wilde of Napiers the Herbalists, and Keith Wray and Tim Hoverd of the Herefordshire Council Archaeology department. I was partly inspired by both the 'onetree project', instituted in 1998 by Gary Olson and Peter Toaig, and the Sylva Foundation's excellent 'OneOak' project.

Joe Atkinson, David Belton, Will Bullough, Joe Christle, Andy Dix, Tom Mareschall, Frank Murphy and Robin Wood all kindly read parts of the manuscript. My agents Claire Conrad and Rebecca Carter of Janklow & Nesbit have both provided first-class advice and encouragement at every fork in the road. At Penguin, Lucy Beresford-Knox, Rosie Glaisher, Richard Green, Rebecca Lee, Ingrid Matts, Shoaib Rokadiya,

ACKNOWLEDGEMENTS

Sarah Scarlett, Sam Voulters and my terrific publicist Annabel Huxley have all been a pleasure to work with. I am immeasurably grateful to my two editors, Helen Conford and Cecilia Stein: their care, erudition and precision have been exemplary.

Finally, finally, I would like to thank my children, who all helped me plant trees to replace the ash I felled. My greatest debt is to my wife, whose enthusiasm for life makes everything seem possible.